TRUE PROSPERITY
ACHIEVING SUCCESS IN A WORLD OF FAILURE

Dallas Humble

PO Box 188 Swartz Louisiana

Published By The Nance Publishing Company
Swartz, Louisiana
USA

©1998 by Dallas Humble

All Rights Reserved. Printed in the United States of America. No part of this book may be reproduced in any manner without written permission except in the case of brief quotations embodied in critical articles and reviews or academic papers and assignments where proper citation of this source must be made.

Scripture quotations in this book unless otherwise noted, are taken from the *New International Version*, Holy Bible.
©1978 by New York International Bible Society. Used by permission.

For inquiries to the author or other information, correspond to Dallas Humble at 3602 Cypress Street, West Monroe, LA 71291. Call (800) 282-1947 ext. 150 to order additional copies of this book

For information on the Nance Publishing Company write to P.O. Box 188 Swartz, LA 71281-0188 or call (318) 343-1130. On the Internet email info@nancepub.com or visit our website www.nancepub.com.

FIRST EDITION

Cover Design by Julia Robertson Nettles II

ISBN: 1-888189-01-0

Printed in USA by Morris Publishing
3212 East Hwy 30 • Kearny, NE 68847
(800) 650-7888

DEDICATION

To my Lord, Jesus Christ for instilling in me the words that made this book a reality.

To my wife, Diane for believing in me and inspiring me to write this book.

Last but certainly not least, to my children, Zachary, Skyler and Payton.

May the words of this book inspire you to live life to its fullest.

I love you.

Contents

Forward vii
Acknowledgments ix
Introduction 15

*Determining Where You Are
and Where You Want to Be*
Forgiving Your Past 25
Recognizing the Present 37
DeterminingYour Future 47

Laying the Foundation for Success
Recognizing and Developing the
   Building Blocks of Life 61
Guidelines for Achieving Success in Business 73
Ten Financial Principals to Live By 85

*Achieving Your Personal Success
and Establishing Your Road Map for Life*
The Boat Without a Sail 103
Charting Your Course 117
Reaching Your Destination 131

Living the Successful Life
Living Beyond Financial Slavery 151
Following the Long and Narrow 169
Personal Guidelines for Sane Living 177

Forward

Fear. Frustration. Fragmentation. Failure. Honestly, what words better describe the overall attitude and mindset of this generation?

Hope, fulfillment, completeness and success are the things for which you and I were created but so few of us seem to find. For whatever reasons, our "world" does not produce an environment that is naturally conducive to the quality of life that we all want.

That's why this book by Dr. Dallas Humble is so significant. It provides stepping stones that guide the way to life as it is supposed to be—life as God intends and makes available for each of us.

I have heard my share of speakers and read my portion of books that have tried to give the answer to humanity's most haunting and unrelenting question—How can I find real meaning in life? I have counseled thousands of individuals, hundreds of couples, and dozens of families who may have asked it in different ways, but the *real* question beneath the question was always the same. You want to know, I want to know, we all want to know, that our life has meaning, our living has purpose, and that our legacy will last.

Though we are all unique creations of God, this is the one universal desire of all mankind. It begins in childhood, blossoms in adolescence, and balloons in adulthood. Life without meaning—without significance—wallows back and forth between drudgery and despondency, never fulfilling and always frustrating. We sit, we soak, we sulk, we seethe, and then we sour. We die—before we die.

In *True Prosperity*, you will find easy-to-understand principles joined to biblical truths that, believed and applied, can revitalize or even revolutionize your life. What you will read herein really does work.

Dallas speaks to us with clarity and conviction because he has lived what he writes. He has been there. He's done that. If his life were a novel, it would be one of the best "success" stories you could ever read. I know. He has been my close friend for more than a decade, and I have personally watched his transformation as he has applied these life-changing principles to his own life.

Wherever you find yourself in life at this moment, this book will be helpful to you. Reading it will be some of the best time you will ever invest in your future.

Michael D. O'Neal
Senior Pastor
Family Church
West Monroe, Louisiana

Acknowledgments

Writing a book is an incredible undertaking, especially if you have never done it before. I believed that through my speaking engagements, seminars and other writings that I would just sit down and write that first book. Well, it wasn't quite that easy.

It's said that you can tell a lot about a person by the company he or she keeps. With the truth I believe that statement holds, I am surely a blessed man. I have been influenced by some of the most wonderful people a person could ever have the privilege knowing. As a matter of fact they are more than I can count, but I want to thank some of them for making this book possible.

First, I would like to thank Tim Nance of the Nance Publishing Company for believing enough in me to take the necessary time it took to make this book a reality.

Specifically, I would like to thank my mother and father for their love, influence and support my entire life. I miss you Dad and am ever grateful to both of you.

I would like to thank my loving friend and Pastor, Michael O'Neal for the spiritual impact he has made on my life. And also I greatly appreciate him for writing the forward for this book.

I would like to thank Zig Ziglar for making such a great impact on me during my formative years through his books, seminars and in every chance that we've had to exchange brief correspondence.

Many thanks to the other wonderful thinkers, writers and speakers, such as Mark Victor Hanson, Ken Blanchard, Brian Tracy and Anthony Robbins for influencing me without realizing it, to reach out and touch others becoming all I am capable of becoming.

Thanks to all the fine men and women who have attended my seminars and purchased my services and products over the years. Your observations have been invaluable to me. You have my unbounding gratitude.

In my company past and present there have been many people who have helped me beyond measure. Although I cannot name each of you of you due to limited space, you know who you are and I do thank you.

My heartfelt thanks to Diane Cleveland and Rhonda Hankamer for staying by me through the hard times. You are both like family. To Drs. Brian Coleman, Adam Karamanis, Bob Rendina and Karri Gramlich for your trust and respect throughout the years, the feeling is mutual.

One of the most important lessons we learn in life is that we are all dependent on others. No one ever does it all alone. There are so many people I could thank but space does not allow it, so let me conclude by thanking my soul mate and wonderful wife, Diane, for everything, but especially the time it took to complete this book. To my dear children, Zachary, Skyler and Payton of whom my world revolves.

And last, but above all to my lord, Jesus Christ, for instilling me the strength, perseverance and wisdom to touch others.

I love you all.

Dallas

Success is not measured by what a man accomplishes, but by the opposition he has encountered, and the courage with which he has maintained the struggle against overwhelming odds.

—Charles A. Lindbergh

Introduction

It seems everywhere you turn these days people are searching for the answers to success in life. We are bombarded with get rich quick schemes. Television ads promote products or services that promise the world. Daily we face decisions that potentially could cause total destruction to our lives. In order to assist you in becoming *successful* we must define what success actually is.

Sometime ago someone asked me what was the key or *secret* to success. My first thought was what did they define success as being? Success is defined today as everything from financial freedom to spiritual fulfillment. For some it may mean money, financial independence and recognition. For others, it just means being *happy* in life.

In all reality, it encompasses all of these factors and more. As human beings we are never really satisfied. When one goal in life is reached, we establish another. If we didn't do this, we would become complacent in life, and our lives would take a turn for the worse.

How do I define success? I define success as being loved by God and having a true loving relationship with him. I believe it means being loved by my family and those I come in contact with during the course of this life. I think of success as having an intimate relationship with my wife, a loving relationship with my children and spending as much quality time with them

True Prosperity

as possible. It means having the financial freedom to do for the ones I love, understanding that without them the material things are meaningless. Last but not least, success to me means being able to enjoy life and the things that are non-materialistic in nature, such as my family, the ocean, the mountains, wildlife, children, laughter and so on.

If success doesn't encompass more than what you can achieve and how much money you possess, you may need to ask yourself this simple yet life awakening question. Is it possible you are too busy doing that you have no time for being? If you honestly ask yourself this question and the answer is yes, don't feel like you are different. Actually, you are like most of the world. We become so busy achieving and pursuing that before long we lose touch with our mortality. Life passes us by, and if we are lucky, one day we wake up. The sad part is that for many in their latter years regret becomes their focus of life rather than a learning experience.

I remember a man in his 30s that was stricken with cancer. While fighting for his life, he felt that all of the things he thought were important in life suddenly had no significance. His life's wish list before was very different. Now all he could write down of importance was his God, his family and his friends. That's it. Yet all his life these things, although important, took second place to the many other things he desired. He later went into remission and to this day has never lost sight of his priorities.

How sad it is that it takes something so drastic to make us wake up in life. Many individuals pursue what they believe is success so diligently that they reach the top of the ladder and find it was leaning against the wrong wall.

Introduction

Am I saying we should never dream, set goals, pursue and achieve? Absolutely not! I am saying that in the process of doing so we need to define what it is we want out of life. I hope to assist you in recognizing and developing these factors in an easy to understand, step-by-step fashion.

As you read this book, I am going to attempt to give you the necessary information and ammunition you need to be successful at life as it relates to these issues and, most importantly, as defined by you. How? Simply by giving you the formula for having victory over your personal life with easy to implement strategies, principles and guidelines. We will discuss determining where you are in life, how to lay the foundation for success and how to achieve it.

Finances and how they affect your life will be looked at in detail with principles spelled out in a simplistic, understandable manner. We will look at guidelines to assist you in being successful in the business world with financial principles to keep you out of financial slavery. There are no guarantees against financial mistakes, but we can through sound biblical principles circumvent financial destruction in most instances if we adhere to them.

I have found that one of the main causes of not achieving and enjoying all life has to offer is being laden with debt to the point you can't seem to see the trees for the forest. It penetrates your marriage, love life, family life, spiritual life, etc., by obsessing your mind 24 hours a day.

It is true that money doesn't buy happiness. Money doesn't buy unhappiness either. What we do with it does.

As we proceed into understanding this and other principles, I feel it is imperative to be sure you understand that although we

True Prosperity

will be focusing on many of the financial aspects of your life from different angles, there is a lot more to achieving true prosperity than money. The Bible speaks explicitly about prosperity in a positive way as long as it's taken in the proper perspective.

We all know the Bible doesn't hold money out as the answer to happiness. As a matter of fact, if we pursue it as our only goal in life, it can cause total destruction by causing us to be its servant. Money is neither evil nor good. It's the love of money that is evil. Money is just currency used to trade for a good, service or item.

No, money doesn't buy happiness. There are many people out there that have little money that are happy and fulfilled. I would venture to say however, that as debt increases out of control, peace of mind and happiness decreases.

We will be discussing the lack of financial control and principles to take control of your assets, not merely control the amount of them. We'll take a look at the way you review life and strategies to assist you in attaining success according to your standards, not the world's. And last but not least, we will look beyond financial and worldly attainment to guidelines for enjoying life to its fullest, learning how to live the successful life from day to day. You may have very little, but if you are fulfilled, in control and free from financial slavery, you are allowed to be the servant, husband, wife, father, mother, friend, leader, etc., you were meant to be. In essence, you are mentally capable of pursuing your dreams. In order to assist you with attaining this freedom, you must first decide you have had enough of the life you are living and be willing to make the necessary sacrifices and changes for this to become reality.

Introduction

As you read through these chapters, please do not skip one to proceed to the other. Each is written as a foundation for the next and ultimately our *house of success* will be constructed on solid ground. You must realize the fact that in all attempts at making it (i.e. business ventures, etc.), there is also a downside to go through. This is one of the biggest mistakes people in business make today. We are ready to try what may sound like a real money making idea and identify all of the steps needed to make it succeed. We have, however, forgotten to look at the downside thereby identifying ways to circumvent failure.

How can I say this so confidently? I can because I made this mistake more than once in life. I now have a plaque on the door of my office that reads, "I do not know the secret to success, but I do know the secret to failure—trying to please everyone!" How true this is. We often are so caught up in a stage of denial. We will go along with a project someone suggested just to please them. But we will not honestly look at how the project might fail. We say, "Let's go for it!" without stopping to plan what to do when the first mountain is confronted. This is true whether it be in our personal or business life.

This downside, regardless of what part of life it relates to, must be examined closely so that we know what to do should it occur and how to circumvent it. Take marriage for example. If we were totally honest with each other prior to making that lifetime commitment, many of life's challenges would become less life threatening. What do you like least about the person you are committing to, answered honestly, may be of more help to you than what you like the most.

This simple evaluation of the downside risk answered honestly goes a long way toward increasing the success of each

True Prosperity

venture we are committing to in life. So, as we begin identifying and learning the principles for taking control of your future, keep in mind that no one said it was going to be easy. Nothing worthwhile ever is. There are bad habits to break, changes to be made and action steps to be taken. The most difficult of all is breaking bad habits that have been formed.

To give an analogy of this, think of the magnificent space missions that were made to the moon. Most of the fuel was used during the initial part of the journey when the rocket had to break the earth's gravitational force. Once that was done, the space travel and return to earth didn't require nearly the amount of energy required during the initial take off.

A habit is the same! Breaking it takes most of our energy. It takes commitment, dedication, persistence and hard work, but after a while it doesn't require the same amount of energy. As time goes on, the energy it requires to keep from falling into the same habit decreases until eventually you broke the habit completely.

There is one thing that you need to do to make the things you desire to happen come to pass. Make the initiative to take control of your future now. If you want to learn something about a specific subject, learn from someone who has already experienced what you want to know, most importantly, someone who has *learned* from the experience.

What I have written is based on personal experiences that I have learned in my life, in hopes of being able to relate what I say. If you like what you read and do nothing, that's the result you will achieve—nothing. If on the other hand, you take what you learn here applying it while using this book as a reference, you will produce results in your life consistent with your efforts.

Introduction

It is my sincere prayer that what I have written will assist you in some small way toward achieving your goals in life, allowing you to experience the success you desire for yourself.

It is not my intent to tell you anything that will emotionally build you up, but rather give you specific action steps built on a foundation of rock to assist you along the way. May God bless you as you take this major step at pursuing your dream and living life the way it was intended—abundantly!

Section One
Determining Where You Are and Where You Want to Be

==Guilt may be part of the past but in order for worry not to consume the future we must be content with the present.==

Not that I am implying that I was in any personal want, for I have learned how to be content (satisfied to the point where I am not disturbed or disquieted) in whatever state I am.

—Philippians 4:11 (Amp.)

1
Forgiving Your Past

INSIDE EACH AND EVERY ONE OF US LIES a part of our self that most of us never develop. It is a part of us that drives us with passion in life that only few portray. The sad part is all of us have this innate "super self" within us. I call it the seed planted by God.

Although we all have this seed, it is up to us to water and nurture it to its full growth. As we proceed, we will reveal how you too can develop your giftedness and have passion and joy for life. Regardless of what one possesses or attains in the materialistic world, if we do not understand the underlying principles, strategies and concepts that lead to a fulfilling, more organized life, we will never find happiness.

On the other hand, you must understand and develop the spiritual side of yourself for you to experience true joy. Joy is what makes life worth living. As we begin learning how to achieve success in life, we must first confront and forgive our past mistakes and those that have wronged us. This is one of the most difficult steps toward having the life you desire for yourself.

Without our past failures we would not be all that we can be. Had I not made the mistakes I did I probably wouldn't be writing this book nor would I have achieved the success life has brought my way. More importantly, I wouldn't appreciate it the way I do today.

True Prosperity

Without life's lessons we would never learn right from wrong or good from bad. A child may be told repeatedly not to touch the hot stove, but unfortunately the word is nothing like the experience. Should the child go against your word carrying through with her actions, you can bet what was learned will never be forgotten.

Like children not knowing right from wrong, we venture through life. We are told, taught, read to, preached to and guided about the right things to do. Yet life is full of choices not always fitting into the box we were given. Our circumstances are different. The people involved are different. We are different. What others have seen and done may be important but the choices that face us are unique. This very uniqueness allows for the mistakes we make in life. We then fail when success seemed so close yet seemed so far. General Colin Powell, whose leadership helped win the Gulf War known as "Desert Storm," once wrote the following.

> There are no secrets of success. Don't waste time looking for them. Success is the result of perfection, hard work, *learning from failure*, loyalty to those for whom you work, and persistence.

We can look at our past in one of two ways. We can be bitter or we can be forgiving. If we choose bitterness, it will cause internal bleeding. We may become bitter towards God, towards our families, loved ones, jobs or even toward the world in general. In essence, our bitterness spreads towards everything and everyone we come in contact with.

Forgiving Your Past

If we choose forgiveness, it will cause external bleeding. When we forgive our past mistakes accepting them as lessons in life, a peace comes over us seen externally by others.

Unforgivingly bitter individuals blame everyone else for their mistake, believing life owes them a favor. The unforgiving individual carries the deposits of life indefinitely.

People walk in and out of our lives daily leaving deposits much like an overhead bird. A bird may fly over dropping a deposit (for lack of a better word) on our nose and fly off.

We can wash our face, forgive the bird and go on. Or we can leave the deposit prominently affixed to our nose for all the world to see. Before long people will start avoiding us. We can forgive the bird or hold a grudge for the rest of our lives.

People are much like this. They carry the deposits of life layering them one after the other. Before long no one cares to be near them. Perhaps you are one of these people. You hate seeing others become successful. You scoff at new ideas, laugh at others and discourage all that come in contact with you. If you are one who has not realized the gift of forgiveness others may view you that way. It is my desire for you to free yourself from your past mistakes or failures thereby taking the first step toward achieving true prosperity in your life.

Occasionally, my wife and I are fortunate enough to travel alone together. It is difficult. Loving our children as we do, we do not like leaving them behind. We do consider sharing time alone important. When we do travel, I am amazed at the amount of baggage that we take. I'm just as guilty as she taking everything in the closet at times. Recently, I took a closer look at the amount of baggage we hauled around. I asked myself, do I really need this? What is its purpose? Would I miss any of it?

True Prosperity

Could I function better without it?

After evaluating the situation, I realized that much of what I was taking was excess baggage. When we arrive it gets in the way. We can't hide it and at times we stumble over it. No matter what we do with it, the baggage inhibits our lives during that time away.

This excess baggage is much like the baggage we carry with us from childhood. Excess baggage comes from lifelong unforgiven deposits. The baggage hinders. It creates frustration and friction. Ultimately the success we desire alludes our grasps. We can forgive or we can continue down the road of unforgiveness, holding grudges toward others and resentment. Forgiving individuals realize that it does no good to hold grudges or resentment in their heart. They forgive and wash the deposits of life clean. The deposits of life are not usually focused intentionally. Even if they are, they are not worth dwelling on.

Forgiving individuals look inside themselves. They accept responsibility for their own actions desiring to allow failures to make them a better person. The unforgiving individual is quick to anger, quick to speak and at times allows hatred and condemnation to build up on the inside. The forgiving individual has a peace inside, peace with others and most importantly peace with God. They have a love for others, are slow to anger, slow to speak and slow to point the finger at others.

James best described this individual in James 1:19, "My dear brothers, take note of this: Everyone should be quick to listen, slow to speak and slow to become angry."

Forgiveness allows us to be thankful we are still alive and have the opportunities lying ahead of us. As good and right as it

Forgiving Your Past

is, however, forgiveness is one of the most difficult things we must do.

Let me give you an example of forgiveness that very few of us could live up to. Terrence Rose, a well-known evangelist and personal friend, tells of a true story dealing with forgiveness that would challenge the best of us. He told of a man who had a next door neighbor that had molested his young daughter. Naturally the daughter's father wanted to kill the man. Attempting to live right his whole life he refrained from physical violence, but never truly forgave the neighbor.

As the years passed, the daughter's father had developed a severe case of arthritis and chronic heart disease. One day looking out the window, he saw his neighbor jogging by. In despair he cried out to God. "Why? I have served you all of my life. This man sins against you and has his health. He appears happy while I am suffering. Why God? Why?"

He suddenly felt an intense need to forgive him and ask forgiveness for the way he had felt toward him all these years.

"Me? Ask for forgiveness? He sinned against me! Why should I forgive him much less ask him to forgive me?"

The answer came clearly. "Because I forgave you."

So reluctantly one day soon after this, he approached his neighbor. Crippled with arthritis the man could not move fast. As he slowly approached his neighbor he began to speak to him. Something he had not done in years. He told him how he forgave him and asked him to forgive the way he felt about him over the years. Almost instantly the man was healed of his arthritis and heart disease. Several weeks later he heard a knock on his front door. There stood his neighbor somewhat emotional. He said, "What you said to me several weeks ago

True Prosperity

touched me greatly. It takes something special in a person to do that. Recently after you said those things to me, I was compelled to go to a local church. I have recently given my life to Christ and I thought you might want to know." This man (the daughter's father) had released himself from bondage and, in turn, touched his neighbor so deeply that he will never be the same again.

What if the neighbor would have not made this life changing commitment? That still doesn't change the fact that the man was released. He is now free from the slavery entrapping him. There are countless stories of forgiveness, but all have a common denominator—freedom. Forgiveness grants freedom from the past that translates to a more fulfilled and prosperous future.

I spent a great deal of my life trying to understand why something so right is so difficult. Sure we can shrug it off by saying the right things in life are never easy. You just have to bite the bullet and go on. Although sayings such as this may be true, they do not help the person learn to "let go."

As forgiveness is the only way of closing the door on the past, you must look at who you are and what makes you tick. Why do some individuals become successful in spite of overwhelming odds. They overcome physical handicaps, poverty, abuse, etc. while others that have everything going for them never really reach their potential in life?

What is the key difference between individuals born of the same family, having the same opportunities, brought up in the same environment, one goes astray, while the other strives for success? They both made mistakes and experienced failures in life. Perhaps both say they forgave their past. This being the case

Forgiving Your Past

and with the choice obviously being ours, what is the key difference? One really didn't forgive? Maybe. It isn't the environment they were brought up in. If these factors are not the key, what are? You have heard it before. I hope to explain it to you in an understandable manner. Without question the key is a positive attitude on life. Without it we will never really reach our full potential. Without a healthy attitude, forgiveness becomes even harder. Christ was the only man who had a perfect attitude. Forgiving everyone, including us, for all of our failures. We are not perfect. Although we can do our best to view things in a different light and try to be all we can be.

One of the ways to do this is by maintaining a healthy attitude. The importance of attitude can be summed up in the following description I wrote sometime ago:

ATTITUDE

The longer I live, I realize more and more the importance of a good attitude. It is more important than money, earthly possessions, education, success and/or attainments. It is more important than your physical appearance, or your skills. It will make or break everything from a company to a home.

We cannot change the past, present or future, but we can change the way it is viewed and by doing so affect the way we are viewed. In reality, attitude is the very essence of the hows and whys of life. When asked how something was accomplished, attitude is a major factor. When asked why him or her and not me, attitude is the major factor.

Although I cannot change the inevitable, I am convinced that life is, for the most part, how I react to it and less of what happens to me. You are in charge of your attitude and therefore you are in charge of your life.

31

True Prosperity

Your attitude is not something that is to be taken lightly. As stated above, it is the very essence of the hows and whys of life. People lose loved ones in ways that could cause the most positive thinking person to go negative. Instead they choose to serve God and mankind even more. They express their love for God through their lives in ways not dreamed possible prior to their tragedy. Yes, they grieved. They could have become bitter as well. But the choice they made was one of forgiveness.

Grieving for the loss of loved ones is normal. It cleans the soul. But, regardless of what the tragedy is, it doesn't have to turn into bitterness, hatred or condemnation.

My past has been filled with mistakes and failures that would have caused many to throw in the towel and give up. Was my reason for not doing so because I am a strong person? Hardly! As a man, I am weak. It is only through my relationship with God that I have the strength to endure. "I can do everything through him who gives me strength" (Philippians 4:13). It is through Him that I can forgive when forgiveness seems impossible.

The attitude I have on life is my choice. You are one hundred percent responsible for you actions. You may be saying, "But Dallas, it wasn't my fault." That doesn't matter. How you react is your fault. Your future and success begins with closing the door on the past. As long as your past mistakes cause you to think of failure rather than success, you will always be anchored to the past. Anchoring happens when we associate an event or person with something good or bad. Until you can close the door and walk away taking with you only the learning experience and not the mistakes themselves, you will never

Forgiving Your Past

reach the success you desire in life. When I finally forgave my past, myself and those involved, my bitterness diminished. As my bitterness diminished, my problems seemed less "life threatening."

I had all of the human reasons to hate people. I had reasons to hold grudges and retaliate. I have personally witnessed people retaliate for getting their car door dinged by dinging the door of the offender. Why? These people came to the point of verbal abuse because it is the way of the world. The world retaliates. It is unforgiving, non-understanding and likes to get back in greater measure. You need to be different to achieve success in life. You need to realize that true forgiveness will come only with a total surrender to God. You simply cannot do it alone.

Now at times I find myself praying for those that I once couldn't bear to think about, much less to talk about. Forgiveness really is the first step. I don't tell you this because it is easy—it isn't. I tell you this to let you know that no matter how big the obstacle, how impossible it may seem, there is always a possibility by relying on a higher source for your strength. Mathew 19:26 tells us that all things are possible with God. All things! No matter how large your problems may seem there is always hope. Always.

You too may be battling with your past. It doesn't matter whether your past is filled with mistakes to the point of feeling like a total failure. It doesn't matter whether you came from poverty or abuse. If you are willing to submit your pride *and* work, anything is possible. A regretful past is usually discussed with phrases such as "Hindsight is 20/20" or "If only I knew then what I know now, I would...." These phrases do nothing

True Prosperity

to further the healing process so necessary if we are to put our past mistakes behind us.

Gain mastery over the tendencies to get back or get even. Don't conform to the world. Romans 12:17-21 says, "Never pay back evil for evil to anyone. Respect what is right in the sight of all men. Never take your own revenge, beloved, but leave room for the wrath of God, for it is written, 'Vengeance is mine, I will repay,' says the Lord. But if your enemy is hungry, feed him, and if he is thirsty, give him a drink; for in so doing you will heap burning coals upon his head." Do not be overcome by evil, but overcome evil with good.

I suggest you read these words slowly again and again. Put names in places they fit and make it personal. Have one goal in mind. The only way to get past resentment, revenge, rage or retaliation is forgiveness.

It is the only cure. Realize that anger is only one letter away from danger. It's like a cancer and it will eat you up on the inside. Close the door on it and move forward. Without doing so, you will never experience the true joy and peace that life can hold for you. By doing so, you will not only experience true joy, you will also be well on your way to achieving the success in life you so desire.

Suggestions on How to Forgive Your Past

1. Pray for forgiveness for yourself and the strength to forgive those that you may have felt bitter toward for so long. Don't just mouth off a bunch of words. Pray sincerely from your heart. God will listen, but he will not make you talk.

2. Write down all things that have made you bitter concerning your past. If you say you don't have any,

Forgiving Your Past

then pray for forgiveness for lying. We all have things we have done in our past we are not proud of. If someone has offended you, write that down also. Write as if you were writing to them. Don't hold back. There is something magical about writing it down on paper. No one is to see it and I do not advise sending it to the other party. Adding fuel to the flame never works. It's like fighting fire with fire.

3. After you have completed number two, go outside and burn your letter. Watch it go up in flames. Pretend that it is your past feelings burning up before your very eyes.
4. Pray for those that have offended you. This has got to be the hardest of all steps. It will help you in ways I cannot begin to explain. Remember it this way, as you pray for those who trespass against you, God will answer your prayers too.

PEACE	F	Chaos
JOY	O R G	Bitterness
LOVE	I V E	Hate
HAPPINESS	N E	Unhappiness
RELATIONSHIPS	S S	Loneliness

2
Recognizing the Present

How many times have you heard the expressions:

>If only I could...
>If only I were...
>I would like to be....

If you haven't, you are either not listening or you haven't heard yourself speak. We all have wished we could look like or do something we haven't done or can't do.

Now understand what I am saying. *Can't* is not a word I use loosely. It is not a word I use regularly. Yes, we have the power within us along with a positive attitude to accomplish what we desire in life. There are, however, some things that go beyond our ability to achieve. You may desire to look like a popular model. You may work diligently at being the fastest or best in a particular sport. Your efforts are not in vain. Although you may never look or perform like the person you idolized, you can become the best you are capable of being. That's the important point.

Be thankful for who you are and what you have today! There was a time in the not so distant past that I was guilty of always wanting more. I always wanted to have what other people had attained. People share with me the resentment they have for others who live dishonestly yet seem more successful. There are honest people that look at the world and wonder why they

True Prosperity

cannot have a piece of it.

I have thought long and hard about this question and believe I have the answer. All of us were endowed with specific talents that, if used properly, can bring us the wealth we can handle. The universe has within it laws or principles that when lived by allow us to keep the benefits of what we so often want to achieve. Many individuals, although not consciously living by their principles, do so perhaps better and more consistently than others who are trying. For instance take the principle of giving. This principle, in effect, states that if we give from our hearts we will receive back more than what we gave. It has been around throughout ancient times and many modern day authors (including myself) teach its effectiveness. It's similar to planting seeds in fertile soil. Sooner or later a crop will grow and you will receive back that which you have planted. This principle applies to all areas of our life not just finances. If you smile, others smile. If you speak, others speak. If you are nice to others, others will be nice to you. As with all principles, once studied, the principle of giving is easy to understand. Yet, good, honest people become frustrated and later disgusted with life because of this one principle. They say they give but their giving is not from their heart. They give only to receive something in return. The law of giving and receiving is as real as the book you have in your hand. As with any law, however, there is a thin line between the right way and what is considered wrong. If I give only to get back I haven't given to give. I have violated the very essence of my giving, which is to prevent greed from entering my heart and to help others.

Another example would be the law of expectation. Our minds are much more powerful than we give them credit for being.

Recognizing the Present

Psychosomatic is a medical term for a disease that actually originated from the mind. If our minds can cause an actual disease process to take place within the body it stands to reason it could work for the good as well. It's important to understand that our expectations should be heartfelt, for the good of ourselves and others. There is an old adage that says, "Don't put the cart before the horse." Likewise you don't achieve success without first having a *success* mind set, belief system or self esteem that you really are successful. If I constantly think successful thoughts, wealth accumulation concepts and *I can* philosophies then soon my actions will speak according to my thoughts. If accumulating wealth is what you desire you will not suddenly develop wealth consciousness or the self-esteem that you are worthy of your wealth by becoming wealthy. It's just the opposite. You develop the expecting attitude by eliminating the wrong from your life and trusting God and the resources he gave you to work with. A prime example of this is the individual that wins the lottery. In most cases he is financially broke after winning millions of dollars because his self-esteem is not adequate to feel worthy of his wealth. He spends more than he has and eventually sabotages his own wealth based on his lack of self-worthiness. Many people attain success. If you are to maintain success, however, develop your self-image to be consistent with that which you have attained. Then and only then can you learn, develop and apply the principles, strategies and concepts that will assist you in being all you can be.

Successful people think successfully. Unsuccessful people think unsuccessfully. Sound too simple? Well it is. Whether you are *good* or *bad* in society's eyes doesn't bring you one step closer to your goals. Living by the universal principles of life set forth

39

True Prosperity

for you to live by does. The person who has what you want may not necessarily be successful according to your terms but that doesn't make him a failure either. Realize who you are, the giftedness you have and be thankful for each accomplishment you make regardless of how small it may be.

Learning to recognize your true gift in life is not as difficult as it may seem. It is that which you have a passion or burning desire for even though fear stands in your way. My passion in life is writing, speaking and teaching. Yet I had difficulty with English in high school and was frightened to the point of physical illness when confronted with public speaking years later. I could have allowed this fear to prevent me from doing what I do best. It was my choice. I chose to confront my fear, which is the only way to eliminate it, and pursue my calling in life.

President Franklin D. Roosevelt once said, "The only thing we have to fear is fear itself." When it comes to pursuing our gift or passion in life, the only thing we have to fear is the tendency to quit. It is always too soon to give in. One of English Prime Minister Sir Winston Churchill's most famous quotes was a speech to a group of young people. He said, "Never, never, never give up." Napoleon Hill once said, "Persistence is to the character of a man as carbon is to steel."

What is your passion? What do you feel that tiny voice inside of you (God within you) calling you to do? Remember, your greatest fear in life is the greatest obstacle to achieving your goals. Realize that fear stands for False Evidence Appearing Real. Once confronted, fear diminishes leaving us with a sense of accomplishment that drives us closer to our passion in life.

Recognizing the Present

It is you that makes the initiative to achieve and attain what you desire out of life. But you can wish for it until your hair all falls out and have nothing if you sit on your backside and don't act. Dream, establish goals for your life and seek a sense of direction to follow. Whether it's to own your own company, be an actor or be the best carpenter you can possibly be, be thankful for who you are and aspire to achieve your dreams.

To never dream, to never desire new things, to never strive for growth is complacency. It is dangerous. To never be thankful for who and what you are today is deadly. Some work their entire lives never stopping to smell the roses, not even weekends. Imagine never really seeing the outdoors on a beautiful day, never enjoying the laughter of a child, never relaxing for one minute until the day of your death.

You may be one of these people. If so, I urge you to pay close attention to the message of this chapter before proceeding to the rest of the book. It is the groundwork before the foundation can be laid for achieving personal success.

Not one day goes by that I do not thank the good Lord above for who I am, what I am and what I have. Am I totally satisfied with my life with no goals and dreams for tomorrow? Of course not! I do want to be thankful for today because tomorrow may never come.

Unfortunately many people live life as if tomorrow will always be there. They look for the bad in everyone. When the wind of life blows along the dust that may blur our vision, many head straight into it without a thought of the consequences. Should the wind cause a rippling of the water surrounding us, many prefer to stir it up more vigorously rather than allow it to calm on its own.

True Prosperity

You and I have no guarantees of tomorrow whatsoever. Those of you having lost loved ones suddenly know what I mean. Life is here today and that's all we are assured of.

Before you go into a deep depression over that, understand that life, if lived as if today is your last day on earth, can be the most exciting and fulfilling experience you will ever have. Think for a moment. What would you do different if you knew today was your last? I'll bet it wouldn't be spent worrying about where your next dollar is coming from and certainly not about what the future holds.

We get caught up in life's fast pace and loose sight of just how precious life is. If it were possible for a person to come back to earth for one day after death, what do you think they would tell us about living life in general? If they had it to do all over again, would they spend more time at the office? How about taking everything more seriously with less fun and laughter? Do you think this would be the advice you would receive? I doubt it. This may be hypothetical, but I believe it does drive a point home.

We would be told to appreciate everyday we have and strive for fulfillment. We would be advised to laugh when something is funny and cry when we are sad. That may sound simple, but some people have difficulty laughing. A lot of people (men in particular) think crying is a breakdown of their masculinity. Nothing could be farther from the truth. Crying is as much a part of our natural emotions as laughing is.

Last, but not least, I believe they would tell us to love one another not only in our hearts and minds, but in our words as well. It's amazing how many people never tell the ones they love the magic three words: *I Love You.* Fathers, mothers, sisters,

Recognizing the Present

brothers, spouses, and even children go to their grave without ever hearing these simple yet so meaningful words, I love you. Sounds easy doesn't it? Yet there have been people that have watched those they love leave this life for the next one never telling them how much they love them. They feel it on the inside and shrug it off with excuses like, "he or she knows how I feel." Maybe they do, but that's not the same as telling them.

Writing this makes me think of my Dad. He's gone to be with the Lord now, but during the time he was here on earth, we had a wonderful relationship. He taught me all I know about being the committed father and husband I am today. For those of you that tell your children how to live and don't live the example yourself, you may as well save your breath. Your children are only going to do as you say if they can see it in action. They need a living, breathing example to model their lives after. Someone telling them not to drink or smoke while holding a beer in one hand and a cigarette in the other has little impact.

While my father was alive, most of those teachings came by how he lived his life, not by what he said. I was, for the most part, bound by verbal restraints. For the majority of our life together I never spoke to him about what he meant to me. At the age of 76—I was 34—he was stricken with terminal cancer. During those last months, I felt as if I grew closer to him than ever before. We spent quality time together, dreamed about things we would like to do and places we would like to go. He was an avid deer hunter and I had just joined a particular hunting club that excited him. I fixed up the hunting camp and prepared it for him although my mind told me he probably not get to enjoy it. Still, I never lost faith.

True Prosperity

I tried all I could find within and without mainstream healthcare to bring him into remission, but it wasn't in the plan of life. On August 14, 1994 he passed away. Just prior to his passing, I was fortunate enough to whisper in his ear, "I love you Dad." I did so twice and he acknowledged me with a facial expression. Although loosing him was one of the most difficult valleys of my life, I realize how fortunate I was to speak to him before his spirit left.

If you have had a similar experience, but didn't have the chance to verbally express your feelings, remember chapter 1, "Forgiving Your Past." Let go and move on. Begin to develop a totally different perspective on life. I have a pact with myself not to speak to my loved ones without saying *I love you*. If I speak to my wife five times in a day, then I will say *I love you* five times. The same goes with my children. Why? Because no one knows what tomorrow holds or whether that will be the last time you see that person. Life is unpredictable.

Simply put in Forest Gump's terms, "Life is like a box of chocolates, you never know what you are going to get." That can be positive as well if we choose for it to be. We can view that challenge as exciting. Live life to its fullest each day we are allowed to see a sunrise or sunset. Express and receive love as if today were the last day we were on earth. Recognizing the present. It's the next step to achieving personal success. Don't let another day go by neglecting to look around you and take in all life has to offer.

Suggestions on Recognizing the Present
1. Keep life in perspective by realizing nothing is more precious than living. Nothing! Should you loose sight

Recognizing the Present

of this, take a walk through a cemetery. This may help you realize that the only thing separating you from joining them is a heart beat.

2. Be happy with who you are. Realize you cannot change the *who* in you. God made you in his own image. Who we are is out of our control. To be unhappy with who you are is a slap in the face of God. What we are is in our control. To be unhappy with what you are is a slap in your own face.

3. Strive to be all you can be by establishing goals (refer to Section III) and committing yourself to them without loosing sight of today. It can be done and although we should live each day as if it were our last, striving to be our best develops a high self-esteem. That's important if we are to be happy with what we are in life. Realize that each day we can be a little more loving, a little more caring, a little more of what our potential in life is, allowing us to truthfully be happy with what we are today.

4. Be thankful. Always have thanksgiving for all you have, all you have become and for the many blessings that have been bestowed upon you. Life can change at the blink of an eye and what you have today could be what you strive for tomorrow. (Refer to Personal Guidelines for Sane Living and make them part of your daily living described in Chapter 12 of this book.)

3
Determining Your Future

As you venture into tomorrow, it is important that you have yesterday and today under control. What do I mean? Simply that, should you proceed into the future with even the slightest bit of bitterness toward your past or a lack of appreciation for today, then your work for tomorrow will be in vain. The past will always haunt you. The present will be meaningless because you do not have the ability to recognize and give thanks for what you have. This is why I have spent the first two chapters emphasizing these points. Now that I have laid the necessary groundwork for moving forward, ask yourself a simple question: Am I willing to take the necessary steps toward changing my life even if it means changing me?

Should you answer yes, you are now ready for the next step toward achieving your dream in life. Changing ones self is difficult. Sometimes it seems impossible in the eyes of the individual. Nothing, however, is impossible if we put our minds to it with the power of prayer. "With God all things are possible" (Matthew 19:26).

Michael O'Neal, Senior Pastor of Family Worship Center in West Monroe, Louisiana, has been a personal friend, spiritual counselor and pastor of mine for years. He once said, "The distinguishable difference between successful and unsuccessful people is that they are motivated by a dream that is bigger than themselves." In order to determine where you want to be

True Prosperity

tomorrow, you need a dream today. In order for that dream to come true, be motivated. Have the faith and know how to pursue it. Make the necessary changes in your life that allow that dream to one day become a reality. Without a dream that encourages a vision and the hope it will come true, a person will stagnate in life. This in turn causes bitterness toward the past and present and the cycle of dreaming or determining where you are and where you want to be starts all over again.

At a very difficult time in the life of Helen Keller she was asked what could be worse than being born blind. Without hesitation she replied, "To have sight and no vision." That's what dreams are made of, seeing not only with your eyes, but also with your mind.

If I were to ask you what you want out of life, you could probably without hesitation tell me your desires, wants and dreams. But if I asked you what had the slightest possibility of becoming a reality, what then, hesitation? Would your wish list be as long as the first?

Dreams accompanied with action are what this world was built on. Can you imagine if you had lived before the invention of electricity or the telephone? Individuals with a vision purused these dreams. What ridicule, condemnation and disbelief they must have undergone. They could have easily given up. They could have given into the world's way of thinking: it can't be done. But they didn't! *Can't* was a four letter word in their vocabulary and four letter words of this sort were forbidden.

Today electricity is so much a part of our life we can't live without it and for heaven's sake, don't take away the telephone. It is the very nucleus of communication today. If these dreams

Determining Your Future

had not been ingrained in their minds with persistence at the core, where would we be today?

Do you have dreams that you believe in, but no one believes in you? Don't feel alone. The only person who knows your dreams is you. You are the only person who can make them become reality unless, of course, someone else thinks of them and pursues them before you. Even so, no one knows your most inner thoughts. No one knows your vision exactly the way you do.

How often have you had an idea that became a dream? You envisioned it. Having a picture of it in your mind, you wanted to act on it only to find out that someone just did.

Remember, many of the dreams you have are probably not yours alone. Others may also have them. The difference is the motivation and the persistence to pursue it to the end. You have dreams. We all do. We have dreams of a new home, dreams of you and your family enjoying a vacation together in a special place. Many have dreams of pursuing a goal in life that you have always wanted but were afraid to try.

Dreams. They make life exciting. They give it meaning. How do we get off course from realizing our dreams?

To avoid this there first needs to be a willing to change and act upon that change in your life. Next, you need to have the vision embedded deep in the recesses of your mind of what your dreams are. Then comes the persistence necessary to make them become a reality.

In between these points are the four *D*s of destruction that cause us to take our eyes off of the dreams that are dear to us. Each is important to understand so that we do not become their victims loosing sight of the dreams we have in life.

True Prosperity

It is important that you recognize these destructive *D*s do not come from God. They are hatched in hell and are present, haunting us in all aspects of our lives. It may be in your relationship with the one you love, with a friend or even with God himself. It may be in your pursuit of success in your life and a dream that you have envisioned for sometime. Regardless of what part of your life they affect, always be wary of their presence. Keep your eyes focused on God for your strength if you are to circumvent their snare and ultimate destruction on your life.

Let's take a look at each in detail as we relate them to our lives. As I list and define them, you will probably see how these *D*s of destruction have affected you at sometime during your life.

The Four *D*s of Destruction

1. Distraction

    As we pursue a goal or dream in our life, one of the first ways we are led down the wrong path is by distractions. Something or someone takes our eyes off of the vision we have established for our life causing us to loose focus. The distraction often seems more appealing, fun or productive.

    In my case, it was the pursuit of the almighty dollar. It distracted my mind from my wife, my children, my friends and even God. The funny thing is you couldn't have convinced me of that at the time. That's how destruction works. It takes your eyes off of where they should be and, without knowing it, places them where

Determining Your Future

they shouldn't be. Now the next *D* of destruction begins its devastation.

2. Deceit

   Once distracted, your sense of direction fools you. You think this new path you now focus on is better. But you are being set up. The distraction allows deceit to quickly set in. It falsely comforts providing all the answers. It reasons and justifies with you that you are now on the right path.

   When I was distracted, it came in the form of a partnership. It seemed to be the thing to do and had glamour written all over it. I believed that if I didn't form the business venture before me, I would miss out on the opportunity of a lifetime. Because we were not equally yoked, we didn't have the same philosophies about business much less life or where we should be 5, 10 or 15 years later.

   Things appeared to be going well. But due to overly aggressive management, overwhelming debt soon surpassed our means to service it.

   We continued growing, justifying every move assuming our assured success. I see this step often among small business entrepreneurs. Every step that increases debt load and cost is justified by how many customers or patients it would take to profit from it. It's fine to be sure your decision is a profitable and correct one. It's another thing to justify it without the first minute of a devil's advocate review.

True Prosperity

Now that I look back, I realize that I had that little "voice" talking to me on the inside, but superficially everything seemed too good for me to listen. If you are confronted with a decision, listen to that inner "voice." Look at the downside should things not work out the way you anticipate. Looking at the downside can, many times, save costly mistakes. We will expand on this in more detail in future chapters that relate to financial matters. For now, understand what deceit is and where it leads if not recognized soon enough.

3. Defeat

The next "D" to destruction is the defeat you will ultimately suffer from. When we are distracted and led into deceit we generally are not aware of what is happening to us. When defeat sets in, it is the first step of realization that we have made the wrong choice. It is during this stage that we see the empty pot at the end of the rainbow.

I first realized defeat in my business venture when debt had accumulated to the point that we could no longer manage it. We were "Robbing Peter to pay Paul." I was always one who lived up to his obligations. The very thought of this broke my very spirit. At that point, all that was wrong surfaced before my very eyes.

If aware of our predicament we can avoid destruction—the next and last stage after defeat. The problem is having the wisdom to turn the right direction before it is too late. By the grace of God and His grace only, I

Determining Your Future

was able to prevent total destruction in my life.

Coming that close to the destruction stage awakened me with a new vision changing my outlook on life forever. I terminated my partnership. Sold what I could sell, negotiated where I could negotiate and called creditors directly and personally. I also took a different outlook on my marriage doing all I could to learn how to be a better husband. Should I not have taken these steps, I would have lost all: my marriage and family, my business and my name. In this life, your name is basically all you have that separates you from someone else. It states whether you can be trusted and whether your word is worth the paper your name is written on.

Defeat is an humbling experience. It takes no preference on whom it strikes. Those with prideful hearts are struck the hardest. I know. I was one of them. The worse thing about defeat is, if left unrecognized, it leads to ultimate destruction.

4. Destruction

This is the last and final stage of the destruction cycle. For those that reach this stage, the lowest of lows and deepest of valleys have been reached. This stage has no mercy and is experienced by those that have made the wrong choices in life and refused to recognize their mistakes along the way. To avoid these progressive stages constantly be aware of your surroundings and those things you come in contact with.

True Prosperity

Furthermore, be willing to admit you made a mistake and make whatever changes are necessary. The reason so many people continue into this stage is because they are not willing to admit they are wrong. They allow their lives to be destroyed by pride rather than face up to a wrong decision. If you review these four stages of destruction, you will see how they relate to all aspects of your life. From distraction to destruction, your life can be affected if you are not continuously aware of happenings around you.

Seeing someone caught in this destructive trap is difficult especially if that someone is close to you. As stated before, these stages can affect all aspects of your life from outside business ventures to extramarital relationships. Once distracted, the grip of destruction takes hold and drives you through the other stages as quickly as possible. At this stage, find someone you can talk to that you trust.

Ask for their support at getting your life back together and holding you accountable. Accountability to someone can assist you greatly in reversing this cancerous cycle.

I fortunately did not fall into the last category, but it takes prayer, hard work, dedication and changing your course to succeed in life. There are times, however, that no matter what we do it seems success is never the end result. Does this mean you can never succeed, that you don't have what it takes? Not at all! It does mean that we are given a vision and dream being endowed with a special giftedness from God. This giftedness has often been described as qualities we can use to do something big for God and, in turn, for ourselves. It is up to us to use that giftedness to the best of our abilities.

Determining Your Future

We can have dreams, but if these dreams are not within the scope of our God-given gifting, we will ultimately fail. Many people try to be like others by coveting their talents and gifts. The sad part is they never find their gift in life and go to their grave believing they are a failure. To try and fail, takes courage. To fail to try takes nothing and leads to nothing.

When I now see someone who has succeeded in life as it relates to a particular vision or dream, I see someone who was willing to fail. Failure breeds success and dreams allow us to have a reason for trying. We all have our different gifts in life. If we are to make a successful effort at determining our future, we need to realize who we are and what we are gifted at. By doing so, we have made one of the most significant steps towards our attaining success in life that we can make.

Look around you. Most people who lack drive or motivation are not sure what their purpose in life is. When asked, the response is usually, "If only I could do this or that I would be happy and motivated." That particular *this or that* is usually what one likes the most in life and is generally a gifted area. Fear and a lack of faith keeps them from developing that talent to the best of their ability. We have all had visions. We have all had dreams. You may have even held one in your hands.

As you set out to determine your future and explore who you are, evaluate yourself deeply. You may be pleased at what you find. We were all given seeds of greatness. It is up to us to determine what they are and nurture them as we would a plant in a garden. It needs to be watered regularly, allowed to receive sunshine in its life and treated with tender loving care. If we fail to do this, the plant dies as will our gift and there-

True Prosperity

fore our dreams.

    Don't let a day go by that you do not give thanks for who you are today. Likewise, don't let a day go by that you do not pray for your dreams, future and the faith to pursue to the end the plan that has been given you. Praying for your dreams, having the motivation and persistence to carry them through and recognizing your giftedness is the key toward determining your life tomorrow. Poetically speaking, I pray the Lord gives you dreams that allow you to fly and the faith to pursue them no matter how high.

Suggestions on Determining your Future

1. Be willing to take the necessary steps toward changing your life even if it means changing yourself. Changing is difficult. Nobody can change you. It only happens if you are the one making the change.
2. Determine your gift in life by evaluating what makes you tick on the inside. What are your talents and gifts in life? Pursue dreams that revolve around your giftedness, not someone else's.
3. Pray. Dream. Remember life without a dream is life without purpose. Envision tomorrow the way you want it to be to the point of seeing it vividly with your eyes closed. Remember, if you can believe it you can see it and if you can see it, you can achieve it. It's your choice.
4. Pursue your dreams. No one said you were going to make them all become reality. However, if you do not try, you do not know how far you can go.

Determining Your Future

SECTION TWO
Laying the Foundation for Success

True success begins with a strong foundation. False success begins with no foundation.

I will show you what he is like who comes to me and hears my words and puts them into practice. He is like a man building a house, who dug down deep and laid the foundation on rock.

—Luke 6:47–48

4

Recognizing and Developing the Building Blocks of Life

LIFE IS MADE UP OF MANY DIFFERENT PARTS. In each of these parts, we find a piece of our life that if left unrecognized will leave us unbalanced, underdeveloped and unfulfilled. As I stated before, my goal for you is that you experience true success, fulfilling your desires and wants while utilizing your talents. However you define success, there are approximately six areas of your life that you need to recognize to achieve it. Our life is made up of these separate and distinct parts that make us *who* we are. These *building blocks* lay the foundation for achieving success. What we do with them makes us *what* we are.

When our life is not balanced, it doesn't flow but instead bounces and jars us around much like an unbalanced wheel on a vehicle. When balanced, it smoothes out, bouncing only slightly with the occasional bump. Those bumps are the ups and downs that make up our life here on earth. Regardless of how developed your life's building blocks are or how successful you are in attaining your dreams, they are still present. I'm convinced though, that if we are diligent in prioritizing and working on these areas of our life, we will

True Prosperity

encounter smaller, less frequent, bumps than we would otherwise.

Although you are ultimately the one that decides what success is to you, it is important that you confront each of these categories of life, opening the door to finding the success you are looking for. By doing so you will also be forced to *develop* your gifts or talents which, in turn, assists you more accurately in planning for your future. As we look at each of these building blocks, understand that they are in no particular priority, with the exception of the first two. I believe that experiencing life-long success may depend in taking each step in order.

Do not be hard on yourself or be fanatical in trying to be perfect in all areas. Our lives always need work and we all lack in one or more of the following six building blocks. You will never be fully developed in your life and you will never be perfect. You can, however, strive to be the best you can be constantly looking for ways to improve yourself.

Let's begin with the first of the six building blocks. I believe this to be most important.

The Spiritual Building Block
This is the part of your life that makes you who you are and ultimately what you are. It is the very being of your identity. If spiritually you are not right with God and fulfilled within, other aspects of your life will suffer. During the introduction to this book I told you that I didn't believe you could find true success without it. Remember?

Look around you. If you see someone that has success financially, but spiritually they are lost and their family values are less than desired, does that individual really have the kind

The Building Blocks of Life

of success you want?

I have met countless people that had the money and recognition so many of us pursue. However when asked if happy, they usually answer no. Why is this? Is it because money makes you unhappy, or is it the fact that their lives are unfulfilled, or without meaning. I'm not talking about the happy front that many people put on only to change behind closed doors. I'm talking about the real you, the you very few, if any, really ever see.

If we were to place what I am saying in question form, I believe it would be asked in the following way: Who are you when no one is looking? Other than when letting your hair down, relaxing, etc., are you at peace with yourself, at home as well as in public? In all of the goals you pursue in life, does the fact that death is the ultimate end of life as we know it here on earth ever enter your mind? And most importantly, if you were to die tomorrow, would you be ready spiritually for what awaits you?

I once heard Zig Ziglar put it in terms we all can relate to in talking about the importance of having our spiritual house in order. He said, "You're going to be dead a lot longer than you're going to be alive." How true this is. Looking around you, however, you would never know it. People are working diligently all of their lives so that they do not have to work their later years. Sadly, many of these people do not place any time or importance in their spiritual life.

If you can't see it, feel it, hear it or smell it, then it doesn't matter. This is much the philosophy today. I'm not saying that this life isn't important. Life is the most precious possession we have. In order to stay fulfilled, however, we need to stay

True Prosperity

spiritually alert, read the book of life (Bible) regularly and worship at the place of our choice on a regular basis.

We need to place emphasis on the real us within this shell called a body. Our spiritual self is, in all reality's sake, what makes us alive. Some of the most successful people on this earth recognize they owe their success to God realizing where true success comes from. There are those who have everything from money to physical fitness to being liked by everyone (social acceptance) that never find true joy and happiness.

On the other hand, I have yet to find an individual that has a true relationship with Christ that doesn't have true joy and meaning in their life regardless of their possessions. I see so many people in this fast paced world worrying about what they will have tomorrow, how accepted they will be or how high they can go, never giving a minute's thought of where they are spiritually. What a tragedy this is.

I remember watching an interview with a body builder on television sometime ago. When asked about his use of steroids, he responded, "I would rather die at 30 and look good, than to live a long life without the physique I desire to have." When death faces this individual squarely in the eyes, I wonder if he will regret what he said. Somehow I believe he will! Mark 8:36 says, "What good is it for a man to gain the whole world, yet forfeit his soul?" No matter how many possessions you accumulate if you loose your soul, you really haven't gained anything. You have actually lost the most important possession you have, yourself!

Focus on becoming all you can be spiritually and watch your life change for the better before your eyes. Will it alleviate all of life's problems? Of course not! What it will do is

The Building Blocks of Life

allow you to place things in perspective, put your faith in God where it belongs and make life's problems appear smaller than before, just the way they should. You may have to be brought to your knees before you are humbled, but remember many people have to be brought lower than others before they look up. Eventually, however, the only direction you can see is up. It's our choice whether we decide to focus our eyes and hearts in that direction or briefly look and allow pride (your ultimate destroyer) to bring you a life of chaos, defeat and ultimate destruction. Matthew 6:33 says it all in a single scripture. "But seek first his kingdom and his righteousness, and all these things will be given unto you as well."

By placing the spiritual part of your life first, you are laying down a foundation made of rock in which to build your life on. Life may huff and puff and blow on your house, but you will remain standing because your life is anchored and built on a foundation of rock.

The Family Building Block
I placed this second because I believe it is just below our spirituality in importance. The family unit is the very fiber of our development and stability in life. I know we all have heard of family values over the years and their importance in our lives.

Politicians have even grasped their importance. Regardless of how structured our government is or how good the people are running it, the family and its values are what separates a moral, God-loving, law-abiding country from another. We can build more jails, have stiffer laws and penalties for criminals, but without proper family teachings from childhood on up, the chances are slim for an individual to be a God fearing, law

True Prosperity

abiding, productive citizen.

So exactly what are these family values we hear so much about? They may be having parents that love God, one another, and their children, laying down all else for their safety. According to Webster's Dictionary (21st Century Edition), a value is defined as a relative worth or a basic principle. I think of it as learning right from wrong.

A family, whether it be a single parent, one child or many children is the most beautiful gift God has ever given us the privilege of having. It is up to us to teach the younger generation the values that we have had instilled in us from childhood.

Some call me old fashioned in the things I am about to tell you. If they make me old fashioned, then I can't think of any other way I would rather be. The following are my personal beliefs on how children should be taught and reared in the home. You may not agree with all of them, but please understand this is how I was reared, it's how my parents were reared and it's how I am rearing my children. I hope they assist you with your family.

1. I believe in children being taught to respect their elders and always answering with *Yes Ma'am, No Ma'am, Yes Sir* or *No Sir*.

2. I believe in discipline (not punishment) and spankings (not beatings) when necessary. I believe that we should teach our children that if they do not follow orders they will have to pay the consequences.

    Many children are told not to do something and when continuing to do it, no discipline is administered. I never believed the saying, "this is going to hurt you a

The Building Blocks of Life

lot more than it is me" until I had children of my own. I believe that, when at all possible, we should not use our hands when spanking. I believe the hand should be for showing love. I further believe that after disciplining our children we should love them and even hold them until all is okay. This way they realize your love for them and the fact that you are not disciplining them because you are angry.

3. I believe in saying *I love you* to your children as often as possible.
4. I believe in hugging your children as often as possible.
5. I believe in having at least one sit down meal together each week to develop the bonding that is lost because of this fast paced society.
6. I believe in coming home every night, unless circumstances absolutely prohibit it. There are legitimate jobs that do no allow this, but in many cases it's because the father or mother for that matter do not place coming home as a priority.

    My children know that if at all possible their dad is walking through the door in the evening to see them. Countless times I have been asked to dinner for business when I refused. There were times when I needed to be somewhere early the next day and although it would be more convenient to spend the night, I chose to stay home. This develops a stability that can't be undervalued.
7. I believe in being a best friend to your children, but remaining their parent. I am Dad and my wife is Mom.

True Prosperity

They do not call us by our first name.
8. I believe in having someone home for your children when they leave school. I know this is not possible in all cases because of work, etc., but it is important.
9. I believe in openly discussing issues such as sex with your children. This is where I may differ from a lot of people, but remember if you don't talk to them about it, someone else will. It's your choice.
10. I believe in praying together. I'll make this brief. A family that prays together stays together.

These are ten personal beliefs I believe to be basic values a family needs to develop into all it can be and stay close throughout life. If you don't agree with all of them, that's okay. A few of them would go along way toward helping this world's families today. One last thing to Fathers, the best thing you can do for your children is love your Mother. Let them see it. You are the example of what they will become.

If you are single and do not have a family, perhaps you have friends that you can develop close relationships with. Regardless of whom, you can have all the money in the world, but loneliness knows no barriers.

The Social Building Block
We have all met people we don't want to be around for various reasons. Let me fill you in on a fact. If you can't get along with people, finding success in life is like looking for a needle in a haystack. Your ability to communicate, like and be liked weighs heavily on your ability to climb the ladder of success.

Count the friends you have in life. If you are stuck on the number zero, then perhaps you need to look in the mirror at

The Building Blocks of Life

yourself. It's been said that you can tell a lot about a person by the friends he or she has.

If you died today, would your name be socially acceptable to pass along to your children? The answer to that question will summarize how your social life measures up on the ladder of success.

The Physical Building Block

You can't buy health. I remember as a young man watching a gentleman that was known for his wealth in life. Basically there wasn't anything that he couldn't purchase. At least nothing that was purchasable. As this individual walked with several other men through a country fair, I could see sadness written all over his face. It was less than one year after that point I came to find out that he had died from cancer. He knew he was terminal when I saw him and no matter what excitement surrounded him, regardless of how much money he had, he was dying and there was nothing he could do about it.

So what's the point of this short story? Without your health materialistic possessions in life are meaningless. Take care of your body. It's the only one you will have. You may not be able to circumvent every illness that comes your way, but you can certainly add quality to the time you have here on earth. Exercise regularly, eat right. Seek out alternative health care providers such as chiropractic for your health needs. You can splurge now and then. But limit caffeine intake and take proper nutritional supplements on a daily basis.

Sounds easy doesn't it? In essence, it is. Don't overindulge regularly and don't deprive yourself of the things you enjoy eating without enjoying them once and a while. Remember

True Prosperity

that success in life is worthless if you are not here to enjoy it. The key is moderation.

The Mental Building Block

The mind is like a muscle in the body. It can be developed if we are willing to spend the time doing so. The world is full of people that have chosen to expand their mind and become knowledgeable in specific areas. Don't believe just because you may lack formal education in a certain subject that you can't learn about it. Success stories abound concerning those that have developed their mind as a bodybuilder does his body. God favors no one. If you believe that, and you should, you will realize that you can become and do what you desire if you have the mindset to do so. In short, read and learn. The mind is a terrible thing to waste.

The Financial Building block

We will cover finances and guidelines to live by in a later chapter; however, you need to face the fact that as important as they are, finances are still only one-sixth of your success. Remember money is only good for what it buys. It's enjoyable to be able to purchase the things you want and desire and live the lifestyle you have always dreamed of, however, happiness is a byproduct of living life to its fullest. Money, on the other hand, is a byproduct of the service you render while living. I once heard a scenario concerning what money could buy that I thought explained its power and most importantly, its limitations. It went something like this:

> Money can buy you a house, but it can't buy you a home.

The Building Blocks of Life

> Money can buy you a companion, but it can't buy you a friend.
>
> Money can buy you free time, but it can't buy you freedom.
>
> Money can buy you a good time, but it can't buy you happiness.

In essence, money with all of its power is equally balanced by its limitations. So what exactly do we do to develop this building block of our life? Realize the limitations of money while at the same time respecting its power. Follow proper, sound financial guidelines while saving on a regular basis. And last but not least, be willing to give on a regular basis preventing us from becoming greedy.

These are the building blocks of life. Look at each area of your life and attempt to maintain the balance that is so important for living. Understand you and I will never be perfect. We are just striving to be all we can be.

5
Guidelines for Achieving Success in Business

WHY IS IT SOME PEOPLE ENJOY MORE FREE TIME, have more money and are generally more successful than someone else in the same business in the same town? What is the secret? Is there a specific formula that anyone can follow that insures success?

I have been asked about success by those in my field for quite some time. Having operated multiple businesses in various locations—some successful and some not—many of the answers have been answered.

We have up to this point covered success in the broad spectrum with the limitation money has on its meaning. Now we can discuss achieving success in business which, many of you want to know. You can do all the right things, balance your life to your best ability and still fail in business. With that fact known, taking note of some specific guidelines to follow in your business life will assist you in achieving your financial goals.

A strategy or plan of action is a must; however, a plan of action will not work for you if you do not take the responsibility of putting the strategy to work. Considering that you are willing to do this, we will examine some specific strategies that are possessed by the most successful business people of today. If there were a secret formula for success in the business world, most who have obtained it would agree that these

True Prosperity

following 12 strategies are the secrets unfolded. Many are short and sweet. But each contains meaning that will assist you by guiding you down the proper path toward achieving success. Let's examine each of these strategies in detail.

Strategy #1–The Willingness to Learn and Change If Necessary
A willingness to learn and to make changes if necessary is one of the, if not the, most important of all the components to becoming successful in business.

Some people with unsuccessful businesses baffle me. They seem so committed to failure by closing their minds to anything that may help them. Whether they be new businesses or existing ones barely making it, they ask questions but do not listen to the answers. Many are convinced that they are already doing things the right way, and what they've read will not work in their business for a variety of reasons.

These reasons are actually excuses in disguise and make evident their unwillingness to learn and accept the fact that their success concepts are actually failure principles. They are usually too prideful to admit wrong, and too lazy to put any successful strategies to work for them. Accepting that we all can learn and improve, and having a hunger for the knowledge necessary to do so is the first step in achieving the success you desire.

Strategy #2–Understanding Your Business, How it Works and Servicing Your Customers
Once you have accepted the first step, understanding your business and how it works is a must.

It may sound simple but I have seen some of the most organized, efficiently running businesses fail. By the same

Guidelines for Achieving Success in Business

token, I have seen unorganized, inefficiently running businesses succeed. What do they attribute that success to? You guessed it, understanding what the customer wants and providing it. Understanding what your business sells well enough to sell it even if it meant you wouldn't get paid for it.

In the health care business, much of our success comes from providing service above and beyond what is asked for. I once wrote an article that was published for the chiropractic profession titled "Why Are Some Doctors Are Successful, While Others Are Not?" The article centered on much of what I am relaying to you in this chapter. Regardless of whether you are in the health care business or some other business the principles are much the same. Deliver a good service that people want and do it better than anyone else.

There are some businesses closing everyday that should not. No one smiles. No one helps you. No one goes out of his or her way. I am convinced that most businesses could prosper if only they serviced their customers properly. I can almost predict whether someone will make it in the business world by talking to them for a short period of time. Next to undercapitilation, I believe poor management (of which good service is included) is the number one cause of business failures. If you don't understand your business, its workings and what it does on a regular basis, perhaps someone else will down the street or around the corner from you.

Strategy #3 – Having Purpose While Staying Focused
Most businesses start with a business plan. It is difficult to get financing without one. In the plan you state the reason your business will exist: to make or service products, service people,

True Prosperity

etc. This is your business' purpose.

As important as it is to understand your business thoroughly and service your customers, it is crucial to stay focused on your purpose and goals to be effective. It's much like practicing what you preach. To understand something is one thing, to live by it is another. It is imperative that you do not move away from your business' purpose. Stick to the basics.

With all the complaints you may hear from customers it's no wonder why people unfocused on their business' purpose suffer from burnout every four to six weeks. Keep your eyes focused ahead and remain on purpose. Read educational material pertaining to your business. Read healthy, motivational articles and books; attend seminars that focus on inspiring commitment to your business, keeping you up to date and ahead of your competition. Above all associate only with people that have the same or similar belief system as you do.

Then and only then will you reap the benefits of what staying on purpose will produce for you.

Strategy #4 – Take Responsibility for Your Business
My business is not doing well because my employees are not doing their job correctly. Things would be better, but people have been sick all over town with the flu, the weather has been bad and no one's getting out, and on and on the list goes.

Although there are certain things that may definitely contribute to the success or failure of your business, you are the one that controls it. The buck stops with you. Just as a parent must take responsibility for his or her children, so must a

Guidelines for Achieving Success in Business

business owner take control of his or her business. To do less than this is a cop out.

Pointing the finger at someone else will not make you a stronger person. Besides, when you point your finger at someone, three fingers are pointing back at you. Take responsibility for all aspects of your business. You will become a better person for it. It can give you the strength to take on obstacles you would have never thought possible.

Strategy #5 – Don't Pay Attention to What Others Say
No one who is successful at anything is going to have good things said about them without hearing negative comments said as well.

The difference between being successful in business or merely mediocre is paying little attention to the negative comments that are said about them. They focus on the business' purpose to exist. No obstacle will get in the way or distract their attention. It's what I call the *Duck Theory*. Negative comments roll off their back like water on a duck's feathers. Business owners that do not hold firm their beliefs and their purposes are easily distracted. Without the *eye of the tiger* they loose sight of their goal.

Think back through history, even into biblical days. With all success breeds jealousy, and with jealousy comes criticism. Don't pay attention to it. Remember, if you are talked about frequently, you're in good company. Being a good person will not stop it from happening. Anyone that has accomplished anything great has been criticized, even Christ himself.

True Prosperity

Strategy #6 – Avoid the Rubber Mouth Syndrome
In short, if you are going to have more customers and deliver quality service, you are going to have to learn to quit talking and start working. Contrary to most beliefs, people do not want to talk about bass fishing, the economy or what is in the news when they are in a hurry. They can do that anywhere. Take for instance the banking industry. People used to go in, have a cup of coffee and talk to their banker—no more. Now they're lucky if you even go to the drive through window because of the computer age. People want fast quality service. It's a fast paced society revolving around service. Either conform or be left out.

Strategy #7 – Take Your Mind Off of the Geographical Syndrome
"Is it my location?" "Do the people here have the money for my services?" "People would not go for that concept or advertisement in my area?" These are typical geographical comments (demographics) of concern. In most cases, the answers to the above are no, yes and bologna.

I wish I had a dollar for every time I heard an excuse that centered around demographics. It all goes back to taking responsibility for your business. Although there are legitimate concerns, they are few and far between. I have seen people succeed in some of the worst locations around.

Years ago, while visiting a successful doctor in California, I noticed that there was little parking available without an effort on the patients part. The office was not located in a highly visible area either. His office, however, was seeing in excess of 2,000 patient visits weekly between all of the practi-

Guidelines for Achieving Success in Business

tioners. When I asked him about the location and parking problem he replied, "I never paid attention to it. I'm not in the parking business." Get the picture?

Let's look at my example. Would you go to a doctor only because he had adequate parking if he were not competent in what he did? I don't think so. Likewise I'm sure most of us would walk further to get superior service. This doctor knew that because of the service his office delivered, people won't care about parking if the service is superior and the product is better than at the mall with a parking garage.

Strategy #8 – Avoid Burnout Syndrome
Everyone needs time off to spend doing the things they enjoy and spend time with their family. Burnout syndrome, however, comes more frequently with the business owner who is in business without knowing where they are going. They have little or no purpose and feel beat-up after several complaints or negative comments from others. For the person who is on purpose and excited about his or her work, vacation time becomes a want rather than a necessity.

Since your family should obviously come before business, and we should all take time to enjoy the things life has to offer, you should schedule time away from the office occasionally according to your needs, but not so often that you can't serve your customers with the service they deserve.

Strategy #9 – You Must Have a Desire to Break Out of Your Comfort Zone
Comfort zones are easy to get into. You work hard for a period of time and reach a certain level of achievement. While

True Prosperity

your business is in the affluent trend, you are excited and have your attention on the goals you had established. Suddenly you reach a plateau and can't seem to get above it. You may fluctuate above it for a short period of time only to return below the magic number, whatever it may be.

Granted, there are plateaus in which you will reach and max out in business. If this is where you are happy and satisfied, fine. However, if you have reached a plateau and desire to grow you definitely can. The key word is *desire*.

You must truly possess the desire to grow because you will be required to go through changes. You may have to add a staff member, work extra hours, add more space and become more involved in the community. Or if you have maxed out to your capacity, hire a manager. Whatever the change is, you must be willing to do just that, change. I do not know of anyone personally who has had success knock at their door or come looking for them. Seek to find and knock for doors to be opened unto you.

Strategy #10 – Establish Goals And Be Committed To Them
There are goals, and then there are goals. The first type is the ones you talk about but never take the necessary action steps to achieve them. The second type is the ones you establish with action steps and commit yourself to no matter what it takes.

Playing in the game of life without goals is somewhat like playing a game of basketball without a basketball, goals or net. You may try to play the game, but you can never achieve anything. Establish your goals. Put them in writing. Commit yourself to them and do not let anything stop you from

Guidelines for Achieving Success in Business

achieving them. You will be amazed at what you can do. We will discuss goals in detail in Section III.

Strategy #11 – Take Control of Your Own Finances
No matter what success principals you establish, the financial aspect cannot be dismissed. If it is out of kelter then the concentration it will drain from you will bleed you of the energy you need elsewhere. The result is failure or success to a much lesser degree.

To design a financial plan does not necessarily mean finding a financial planner. It means to *take control.* Learn all there is that you need to know.

Establish good spending and saving habits. Set out to learn all you can about how to handle money. Remember, no one is going to look after your money like you will. Learn to take control of your own finances. We will look at specific financial principals to live by in Chapter 6 of this section.

Strategy #12 – Be Willing and Prepared to Work
Last but not least, be willing to work for what you desire in life. As stated before, success does not generally knock on your door. For the few that receive it by lotteries, inheritance, etc., many times the result is disaster, failure and unhappiness beyond comprehension.

Unless you have learned the value of a dollar and what a true work ethic is all about, success will always be waiting for you at the other end of the rainbow. But, if you put these components to work for you and commit yourself to working for your goals, success is sure to become a reality.

True Prosperity

Whatever your definition of success is, remember this: *Believe and achieve, doubt and do without.* If these strategies sound simple to you, remember the simple things are put here for the wise man to see. Wise up and you too can accomplish things in your business and personal life that you may have thought were not possible.

Guidelines for Achieving Success in Business

6
Ten Financial Principals to Live By

Have you ever stopped to examine where your financial life is heading? Many of us have no idea where we are financially. Most of us know, I am convinced, that although we are all human and will make mistakes, experience is a nasty teacher. We know that we are in debt, have bills to pay, and many times don't have money left over at the end of the month. But when asked what is their net worth, many honestly couldn't answer because we would rather avoid thinking about something that has gone out of control.

Every day we all learn what works and what doesn't work in the financial world through trial and error. Wouldn't it be better if we were taught sound financial principles from childhood that if followed would assist in avoiding many costly mistakes. The principles I have laid out for you in this chapter are aimed at doing just that. Without these financial principles and a financial plan, we can become extremely frustrated with life.

For years concentrating on ways to expand my business and better my financial life, I faced many questions. How can I reach more people? Should I add more employees? Should I do more advertising? Should I sign that note? How much should I give and save? The list goes on and on.

All of these things are important. However after many years of business and expansion, I am convinced that without a

True Prosperity

financial plan, you are lost. There is nothing more devastating to one's life than financial strain. It permeates all other aspects of your business, personal and marital, and even spiritual life. your ability to concentrate on anything else greatly diminishes.

What I am going to tell you in this chapter is not a revelation or anything you possibly haven't heard before. We are going to review several biblically financial principles that can prevent many financial mistakes. Hopefully we will discuss them in a way you can understand and use in your life. Regardless of whether you are in business for yourself, working for someone, a doctor, lawyer, CPA, or otherwise, you will find these principles are basic and simplistic in nature.

Although success is much more than wealth, the financial building block of your life needs to be in harmony for you to function productively. That is not to say you have to have a lot of money to be successful. But if you violate certain financial principles, the rest of your life may suffer as well.

There are literally thousands of financial planners who would love to assist you along the way, but many of them can't handle their own finances. This brings us to the first of ten principles we will discuss:

1. Do not trust your finances to someone who cannot control their own.

This includes financial planners, certified public accountants, bookkeepers, insurance clerks, and so on. I personally have *succeeded* exceptionally in this area, which gives me the right to claim it as one of my financial principles to live by.

I had a "financial adviser" who was very intelligent and could literally charm the money right from your bank account. To top

Ten Financial Principals to Live By

it off, he had more than 20 close acquaintances and friends that were clients of his. I used this guy for everything. He invested my money, negotiated any purchases I made, corresponded with my CPA and handled our company retirement plan. My early practice was richly blessed, and in turn so was my *financial adviser*.

After spending many thousands of dollars and enduring years of frustration over not having any money (liquid money, that is), I began to question this adviser about where I was headed. He replied with the same old song and dance about how it takes time to accumulate wealth. He explained that he had no control over what congress did or the new tax laws. All the programs we were in were very solid, he said.

To make a long story short, I lost practically everything. My retirement plan was gone. I watched several close friends and colleagues file Chapter 7 bankruptcy over the years. I barely circumvented that myself.

My CPA was honest and extremely intelligent, but he couldn't handle his own finances. He was always needing money, always behind and always owing taxes! This was not a comforting feeling to have about a CPA.

My bookkeeper didn't pay our bills on time because she didn't pay her own bills. How can you expect someone to handle your finances that can't handle their own?

None of these people are with me now, but I had to learn this the hard way. Take my advice: ==Only deal financially with those individuals who have their own financial house in order.== How do you find this out? Ask around, do research and do whatever you have to do, but find out.

True Prosperity

I'll give you one for instance that should have caught my attention years ago concerning the previously mentioned *financial adviser*. I can never recall having any liquid cash saved in any of my accounts. When I asked him the question, "You must have cash saved; why shouldn't I do the same?" he answered, "I have very little cash. I have all my money 'working' for me, not just sitting around 'stagnating.'" Get the picture?

This brings us to my second principle.

2. Never invest in something you do not understand yourself.

This is something that came somewhat easily for me, although late. After all I had been through, I joined several financial organizations, attended seminars, read books, listened to tapes, watched videos and read every article I could get my hands on that dealt with finances. I wanted to know it all: bonds, stocks, mutual funds, annuities, life insurance, retirement plans. I was like a sponge. I felt like I had betrayed God by not handling what He had blessed me with properly.

After learning, I began to make intelligent decisions on my own, or with the help of someone who thought the way I did. I was amazed at what I learned, and at what I had invested in prior to that time.

Did you know that, with a little time, you could become as knowledgeable about most basic money matters as the majority of those who hold themselves out to be financial planners? Many people are skeptical of this and will pay exorbitant fees for investments they could have chosen for themselves.

You can read about research that has been done in this area in most financial publications. Peter Lynch, a former invest-

Ten Financial Principals to Live By

ment adviser for the Magellan Fund with Fidelity Investments, has written a book titled *Beating the Market*, where he proves this through several different examples. If you are not convinced by what I am saying, buy his book and read it.

Please don't misunderstand me. There are good financial planners who can help you greatly. It's similar to any business, however, there are many bad ones as well. If you have people handling your finances, be sure you understand principle number one. Go one step further and educate yourself in your own financial matters. Remember, it's up to you to make the ultimate decision. It's your money, and no one is going to have the same concern about it that you will. By educating yourself, you, too, may be amazed at what you can do.

3. **Before you can accumulate real wealth, first get your tax life under control.**

Too often people, myself included, think they are getting ahead and then get slammed between the eyes with an unexpected tax bill. With inevitable tax rate increases, it is even more important that you understand taxes and tax laws. Don't just rely on your tax advisor who is there to file your taxes. Granted, some CPAs may assist in planning, but it is up to you to put aside the money for taxes due and provide the necessary information and documentation regarding your tax status. It is important that you monitor your financial statements and status throughout the year. Why? Because you can't know where you are headed if you don't know where you're at.

Remember that the profit figure is what you pay taxes on. It has nothing to do with how much money you have in the bank.

True Prosperity

I know this sounds simple, but I wish I had a dollar for each time someone said, "How can I owe that much when I don't have any money in the bank?"

Sit down on a regular basis (at least quarterly) with your tax advisor and discuss where you are tax-wise. Learn to read your statements and calculate your approximate taxes due. Open an income tax account and place that amount in daily.

In the past I found it difficult to pay both income and payroll taxes because of a lack of funds. While a business is in an expansion stage, cash is a rare yet welcome asset. I had to find a way to save for taxes and thereby have the money available when necessary. In order to do this, I opened an income and payroll tax account. We placed a dollar amount in the income tax account daily, based on our taxable income as well as a calculated amount for payroll taxes. If you are not self-employed, this is obviously not necessary. But you still need to stay up to date on your tax deductions and tax rate to be sure the correct amount is being deducted from your check.

Always reevaluate this regularly to be sure you are not behind or too far ahead. If you are self-employed and you have specific accounts designated for taxes (i.e. income, payroll, etc.) be disciplined and understand that the money is no longer yours to spend. The advantage of doing this is that you have designated, or earmarked, this money, and it will not be spent for anything else, no matter what.

These are things you will have to adapt to your individual circumstances. They do work and may save you an enormous amount of grief in the long run. Whether you use these specific items to assist in handling your taxes is not the issue. The issue is that you need to face up to the fact that taxes are a part of life and make this consideration an integral part of your financial plan. Without doing so, you may find yourself pursuing a goal that you will never reach.

4. **Never invest your money in something you don't know how to get out of if the cash is needed.**

In other words, steer clear of non-liquid investments as much as possible. I can't tell you how miserable my life was because I violated this principle. If I ever needed money I was told I couldn't get it because it was fully invested. We would have to find someone to buy my investment (i.e. limited partnership, etc.).

There are certain liquid investments that may decrease in value if sold prior to maturity, and there are also certain non-liquid investments, such as real estate, that although are illiquid in nature, have made many investors wealthy over time. That's well and fine. Keep in mind, though, there are many more that have made investors poor. I happen to like real estate as an investment as long as I am confident of the area and potential for income or a quick sale. Just be sure that regardless of what you invest in, you know where the back door is, how to get to it and what it entails. Circumvent as many surprises as you can.

There is nothing more devastating than to find out that your hard-earned money is in a "non-liquid investment" that you either can't get to, or lose a significant amount in principal to get bought out. By educating yourself and becoming involved, you may continue to make mistakes and perhaps even lose money from time to time. But the advantage is that you will generally know what you are investing and help you weigh the

True Prosperity

associated risk. That in turn can save you from making a financially devastating mistake.

5. Give a percentage of your money regularly from your heart.

The fifth principle encompasses all you are made up of on the inside. It really outlines your true purpose for accumulating wealth. Without it, money leads to greed, and greed leads to self-destruction. The Bible tells us that "the love of money is the root of all evil." It doesn't specify money itself, but rather, the love of it. Think of what that says. Practically all corruption in this world revolves around money and the power it brings to those who have it. Don't fall prey to it.

Learn and live by this principle. What I find most interesting are the books published by authors discussing this principle as if it were something new. They explain it and relate it to planting the seed in fertile ground and watching it grow otherwise known as seed corn. *The Richest Man in Babylon* by George S. Clason discusses this principle. Many other famous authors discuss it but the point is that it's a principle that anyone who has read the Bible understands the principle of tithing practiced in ancient Bible days.

Many authors discuss this principle as a way to feel better about yourself. One Christian author discusses this principle as a way to receive one hundred fold return on your giving. Both, in my opinion, are wrong. Giving should be from the heart with no expectations in return. Will you be blessed for it? When you give from your heart for the right reason, yes, but perhaps in different ways.

Ten Financial Principals to Live By

Many people have become turned off to tithing and giving regularly with their money because they don't trust churches, preachers, charitable organizations and the like. Yes, it's important to give to a source that you believe is making every dollar count, but, believe it or not, it is not the most important thing. The most important thing is giving. This principle works, and it works every time.

For example, how can you develop greed in your heart if you give 10 percent or more of your income on a regular basis to your church as the Bible teaches? The answer? It's difficult, if not impossible. I have seen greed destroy people who had the potential to do well with their lives. Families have been lost, relationships destroyed, jobs lost, and financial bankruptcy filed in almost every case. All because of greed

There is nothing wrong with doing well for yourself. It has been said that money doesn't buy happiness. I agree with that wholeheartedly. Happiness needs to come from the heart. I also believe, however, that the lack of money doesn't buy happiness either. Maintain a proper balance in your life. Read regularly for your mind. Exercise regularly for your body. Spend time with your family. Worship regularly at the church of your choice for your spirit. And last, but not least, make financial matters a part of your mental education.

Someone once told me that investing properly is not important. It is not if: (1) giving isn't important to you; (2) spending more time with your family isn't important, and (3) being able to say one day that you are working because you want to, not because you have to, isn't important. It's only important if you want those things. Do you? You are the only one who can

True Prosperity

answer that question. I thoroughly believe you have control over your own destiny. Make the decision to take control.

Here is some food for thought that was told to me some time ago: Life isn't easy. As a matter of fact, it is downright difficult. But, if you are tough on yourself, life is going to be a lot easier on you.

6. Save 10% of your income, regardless of your age.

You want to retire one day or at least be able to? Unfortunately, just working hard is not the answer. As important as it is, you have to save money in order to have it.

It's a funny thing; I've seen people who earn low- to mid-six-figure incomes annually that have less money saved than people who earn less than $50,000. Why is this? The answer is simple. The individual earning the larger income is not frugal with his or her money. There's always tomorrow, therefore, saving today is not necessary. The individual making a lesser income in this case scenario is concerned about saving for tomorrow, not spending for today.

Saving money may seem difficult now. If you can't save 10%, begin with 5% or whatever you can. Take it off of the top before you pay anything else. There are many savings institutions, mutual fund companies, etc., that have low minimal initial investments and will automatically draft your account on a monthly basis.

Take advantage of tax qualified savings plans such as IRS's, 401K's, etc. Remember, it's not what you make, but rather what you do with what you make that counts. Begin making your hard earned money count today. Start saving and watch

Ten Financial Principals to Live By

your financial future grow.

7. Live by a budget regardless of your income.
Have you ever wondered how people who make exorbitant incomes go bankrupt? It happens everyday. You see individuals on television, celebrities, etc. filing Chapter 7 and companies filing Chapter 11 that are all making large amounts of money. Why is that? There are a variety of reasons and although some are legitimate, many are excuses for not taking the responsibility to budget themselves and adhere to it. From something as large as our federal government to something as small as a single individual, without a budget, financial chaos is the ultimate destiny. It's really not as complicated as it may seem.

To establish a budget, first look at what it takes you to live and operate per month. On a personal basis you can categorize each area with the maximum amount you wish to spend per month. Each time you make expenditures toward these items (i.e. groceries, etc.) you can indicate the amount on the budget sheet. At the end of the month you can easily see where your money has gone and what areas, if any, you need to cut down in. Don't forget to include principles numbers 5 and 6 to your budget. There are several good software programs on the market that will assist you in doing this. For those of you who wish to do it manually, that's fine. Whatever method you chose, be disciplined with it.

As for a business, your monthly Profit and Loss sheets from your tax advisor is your Bible of operations. Not a month should go by that they are not reviewed, implementing changes where and when necessary. You can even go one step further as I have in my business by taking your last 12 months average

True Prosperity

from each category and placing someone responsible for each of them. Purchase orders should be signed before ordering items, materials, etc., by the department head. That individual in turn is responsible for his or her department.

If you are a small business the department head may be you. Regardless, of whether it's home or business, someone is required to be responsible for expenditures. Last, but not least, you absolutely, positively, need to get your tax life under control. This was covered in the third financial principle and cannot under any circumstances be overlooked. Summarized, don't spend more than you make and separate tax money from your money. Understanding and living by these two simple yet life-changing statements can make the difference in your financial statement.

8. Don't co-sign or guarantee a loan unless you are willing to pay for it yourself.

I can't tell you how many times I violated this principle. With one exception, I paid for it every time. This single principle can bankrupt you if violated regardless of how well you adhere to the other nine. The Bible itself is explicit about the guarantee of another's debts (Proverbs 22:7).

I understand there are times when a moral obligation seems to overwhelm you and take precedence. Look at it this way. Most of us could not have received credit on our own without the assistance of someone else, someone who believes in you. However, should you be asked to help with a certain debt, face the fact that you are responsible and you have no rights to ownership in most cases. In other words, if you co-sign for an automobile and the loan is defaulted on, you pay and you don't

Ten Financial Principals to Live By

own the car.

The same is true for most guaranteed loans. I'll tell it to you the way I was told when I first asked for assistance. "Start out slow. If I help you this time I expect you to live up to your obligations. If you do not, you will not get another chance. This is your chance to prove yourself. Do not mess it up."

Obviously I am not suggesting you should co-sign for anyone. I am, however telling you that I know most of you will, whether it be for a son or a daughter in need or someone close to you. Inevitably, you will be asked. Weigh the odds. Look closely at the person. Do not hang yourself out or jeopardize your financial status and if at all possible try not to do it at all.

9. Never make business decisions under pressure.

"This is the last one at this price." "If you buy it today, I'll knock off this amount." "You must make a decision now." "I'm glad you came in today. This is the last one of its kind."

These are but a few of the statements made that place a person in a situation of an immediate decision. With the exception of a few cases, I have yet to see a correct decision made when under pressure. Anything worth buying, investing in or contracting with is worth waiting for. Good business decisions require knowledge about the subject that, in turn, requires time. Remember, there is always tomorrow, always another car, another deal, another house, another whatever.

I have taught my children a simple yet meaningful prayer that we made part of our daily prayer together for years. "Lord, help me to make the right decisions when faced with choices." At 4 years old, it may not have a lot of meaning, but

True Prosperity

it will. Perhaps we all could use a little help with our decisions. I know I do. Make patience and prayer an integral part of your decision making process. When pressured with no way to turn, walk away. It may be the best decision you'll ever make.

10. Prioritize extra cash: give some, invest some, and pay extra on debts.

Sound simple? It is, but it requires discipline. Don't just say you will do it. Make it a law. It's just too easy to receive an extra $100, $1,000 or more and think about the things you would like to buy first. If you have money left over after dividing it, then by all means buy something. If not, save it for later.

Regardless, if you follow this simple rule, you too will see your net assets grow. You'll feel good about yourself and the decisions you make as well.

Ten Financial Principals to Live By

Section Three
Achieving Your Personal Success and Establishing Your Road Map for Life

To have dreams is good. To make plans and act on them is better. To believe and have faith, however, is the very essence of success.

Commit to the lord whatever you do, and your plans will succeed.

—Proverbs 16:3

7
The Boat Without a Sail

I ENJOY SPENDING TIME WITH MY FAMILY ON THE BEACH. It's a time that I can relax and enjoy quality time with those closest to me. It is also a time I can develop some creative thoughts.

One day while I was on the beach looking out over the emerald gulf waters, I saw several sailboats drifting at sea. As the wind went down and the sea became calm there was nothing for them to do but sit and wait for the wind to pick up. The sailing term for this windless time of drifting is *irons*. As these boats sat in *irons*, I could imagine the people's frustration grow.

Many frustrated goal setters come into *irons* drifting along without a sail. It's obvious that this person couldn't make the boat move without the help of the wind. The thought soon came to my mind, how then can you successfully meet a goal without relying on God's guidance to assist you along the way?

Setting goals is something practically everyone has done before. Successfully meeting them is something very few do. Why is that? Some say it is because only certain individuals are given the gift of achievement. I believe it's more than that. There are several goal destroyers that we as individuals must face and overcome if we are to do what it takes to make our goals become a reality.

The first is fear. The fear of failing or being rejected continuously haunts us from becoming all we can. Your greatest obstacle to success will, many times, be your greatest fear in

True Prosperity

life. If we think of failing as a means to discover a way something doesn't work, we can approach it in a totally different light. Successful goal achievers all have this trait in common. When asked how many times did you fail they will reply that they didn't fail, they just found ways not to do it again. Failure breeds success. To try and fail takes courage. To fail to try takes nothing and leads to nothing.

Paul Harvey put it best when he said, "Someday I hope to enjoy enough of what the world calls success so that somebody will ask me what's the secret of it?" I shall simply say this: I get up when I fall down." There are success stories after success stories that deal with individuals striving to achieve a goal in life when failure seemed inevitable. One of my favorites dealt with a famous person who lived in the 1800s. It goes something like this:

    1831 Failed in Business
    1832 Defeated in Legislature
    1833 Failed in Business
    1834 Elected to Legislature
    1835 Fiancé Died
    1836 Suffered a nervous breakdown
    1838 Defeated for speaker
    1840 Defeated for elector
    1843 Defeated for land officer
    1844 Defeated for Congress
    1846 Elected to Congress
    1848 Defeated for Congress
    1855 Defeated for Senate
    1856 Defeated for Vice President
    1858 Defeated for Senate
    1860 Elected President of the United States

The Boat Without a Sail

As you can see in the life of Abraham Lincoln failing and being rejected in life is part of the journey toward goal accomplishments. You might say without failure there is no success because the failures are what our successes are made of.

The second goal destroyer is procrastination. Most people mean well but simply do not follow through or carry out the things necessary to accomplish their goals. Procrastination destroys dreams and when dreams are destroyed people are destroyed. Procrastination leads to complacency and complacency is what is left of a person who believes he is satisfied where he is in life and because of past failures is afraid to step out of his comfort zone. The cure for procrastination is simple yet extremely difficult for those who encounter it. Those who have overcome this deadly goal destroyer have understood the cure from trial error. It is to do or act upon whatever it is you are confronting. Nothing will happen unless you make it happen. You are the one that must act and do the things necessary to achieve your goals and ambitions. God will guide you but you and you alone must make the journey. "Well," you may say, "someday I will." I call that the goal achiever's death rattle. *Someday* leads to the land of nowhere and the land of nowhere contains nothing. Be aware of these goal destroyers and do not allow them to keep your goals from becoming a reality. It truly is up to you.

In this chapter I wanted to show you not just to set but follow through on your goals. I could do this but if you do not set realistic goals no one can help you.

Look around you to see what I am saying. I see people establish goals that are no more designed for them than a goal to look like Arnold Schwarzenegger would be for me. I work out

True Prosperity

hard, watch what I eat and try to take care of myself. However, my genetics are not such to naturally grow to his size. Is a goal to look like him designed for me? Of course not! On the other hand a goal to be a certain weight, a certain size (within reason) and maintain physical fitness is a goal that could be tailored to me. So before we go any further, you must ask yourself a few simple questions.

First, are my goals in life spiritually sound? In other words, are they in line with my beliefs and desires in life? Second, am I willing to make sacrifices to achieve them? And third, do I have the persistence to keep my eyes focused when the world is constantly distracting me? Without a *yes* answer to each of these questions, you have already started with two strikes against you.

As someone who enjoys the sport of shooting, I admire a good marksman. I have watched individuals with a steady hand never miss on the sporting clay course or consistently hit the bull's-eye at the rifle range. If I told you that I could show you how to out shoot these individuals in one day, your response might be "yeah right Dallas." But, if you're physically capable, I can guarantee you that you can out shoot the best of them. How? Blindfold the one you are shooting against! Why that's silly! How could anyone shoot consistently when they are blindfolded? They can't even see the target! That's correct. Now, here's a profound question for you. If you can't hit a target you can't see, how can you hit a goal that's not realistic? The answer—you can't. As a matter of fact you can't hit a goal not designed for you anymore than you can travel to a place that doesn't exist.

Unless you have a definite plan of action, you will never reach your maximum potential in life. You will never make it

The Boat Without a Sail

drifting in the *irons* of life. You must establish a target, take aim and fire ahead like a bullet without looking back.

You must be specific. You can't be fuzzy or general about your goals. Saying I want to lose weight is general and fuzzy. Saying I want to lose weight by the end of the year is clearer, but still general. Saying I want to lose 25 pounds by a specific date is clear and specific. You must, of course, have action steps to follow to make it a reality.

We will discuss establishing goals in more detail later, but for now I hope you get the picture. Most of the time a goal when pursued and given up on was only inches away from attainment.

That reminds me of a story told by Napoleon Hill years ago. He told of a man by the name of R.U. Darby from Baltimore, Maryland that mined a gold vein following it to a point that eventually came to an end. After attempting to find the gold vein he decided to call it quits and sold the gold mine to a junk dealer. The junk dealer hired a mining expert that evaluated it and told him to keep digging. Three feet further he picked up the gold vein and it became the most profitable gold mine in the West at that time.

It takes persistence to reach our goals and at times it may seem like quitting is the thing to do. Anything worth having is worth working for. We must keep our sails in life up at all times, keep focused on our goals and allow the breath of God to push us toward our destination.

Often we depend on ourselves to bring us through. True, we must believe in ourselves; however, if we do not humble ourselves to a power greater than ours, we will ultimately be humbled. You can climb the tree of life, but be cautious how

True Prosperity

far up you go without submitting to God as your strength. Should your ego and pride take over, the tree may shake and you will fall a long way down.

We all need help to keep focused and moving in the right direction. We also need to help others. People are all made different. Some need more help than others. Some seem to need little help. Regardless, we all need each other in difficult times as well as the times we are strong. As we travel the road of life, we will all at some time or another drift at sea. But if we have a plan of action and others to lean on and hold us accountable we can accomplish more than we ever imagined.

Now that we have introduced goals and the devastating effects of drifting at sea, let's examine their importance in your life.

In life we will find ourselves drifting at sea. But if we have a plan of action and others to lean on and hold us accountable we can accomplish more than we ever imagined.

Now that we have introduced goals let's examine how to determine if your goals are designed for you. As I explained earlier, you cannot attain a goal in your life that is unrealistic to you as an individual.

I see people establish goals to be something they are not or do something they are not physically capable of doing. New businesses have started and failed with goals of making millions the first year. There is nothing wrong with establishing goals that are large but they also need to be realistic. I have seen countless individuals give up on a specific goal because of confusion and frustration that perhaps with some fine-tuning could be tailored to fit them. This frustration comes from not only missing a goal but falling so far short of it that is seems like establishing and working toward it was a waste of time. For instance, people will claim they are going to lose weight. They follow all the proper criteria for establishing the goal (i.e. specific time, action steps, etc.) But then they set the amount to lose so high that although they were losing weight they quit because they were so far from their goal.

So how do you tailor a goal for yourself? First, you must submit your goals to God and be sure they are biblically sound by asking yourself the following questions:
1. Do my goals inflict pain (physically or emotionally) on anyone?
2. Will my goals cause me to turn my back on God by placing their accomplishments and attainment higher than He places on my priority list? In other words, are my goals so important that nothing else matters?
3. Does praying about those goals cause an "uneasiness" within my spirit?

If you answered yes to any of the above, then you should reevaluate your goals and desires. A goal should be a target that you strive for that has the ultimate outcome of bettering you and those you come in contact with based on your improvement.

Look at yourself from the outside in. By pretending you are someone else, you can see flaws in your desires that you normally would not. You have experienced this with others. Has someone ever told you something they were striving for that you knew was not in their best interest? They, on the other hand, based on emotional naivetes, are blinded to the world of reality only to find disappointment during the journey from here to there.

True Prosperity

Use this phenomenon to your advantage and take an objective view of yourself. If you cannot, then find someone who has your best interest in mind that you can trust his or her opinion. Regardless, it's an important part of being sure this goal's for you!

Now let's take an example of a goal on loosing weight and see how we can take a good goal on paper and turn it such a way that its design is no longer tailored to the individual. Jane, a young girl approximately 22 years old, wants to lose weight. She has all the criteria down for doing so. The goal is as follows:

Goal:	Lose 15 lbs.
Time:	2 months
Action Steps:	Low fat/low calorie diet with specific foods to be avoided. No snacking, no eating after 6:00 p.m. Drink at least 8 glasses of water per day.

Sounds good so far doesn't it? Now let's take a look at Jane presently:

Present weight:	100 lbs.
Height:	5'5"
Self-esteem:	Low (believes it will be better if she would just be thinner)

Now what's wrong with this picture? Does this young girl need to lose weight? Let's take the test to find out if this goal is designed for her:

1. Does this goal inflict pain on anyone?
2. Will this goal cause her to turn her back on God?
3. Would praying about this goal cause an "uneasiness" in her spirit?

The Boat Without a Sail

I believe you will agree with me that the answers to the above are an obvious yes, yes and yes. First, the goal would inflict pain on her by physical damage based on the fact she would have to literally starve to lose this weight. She is already thin (possibly too thin) as it is. Furthermore, her parents would be emotionally harmed from her actions. Second, she would turn her back on God as a priority in her life because she would be causing damage to her body and doing something that is wrong from all angles. Its importance to her would be too great. She would literally have to turn her back on her parents as well. Lastly, could she pray for this goal without an "uneasiness" about her? I doubt it.

Now let's have her look from the outside in. We don't have to spend much time on that one, do we? Anyone with our best interest in mind would say it's wrong: don't do it.

Do you see now how you can establish goals that are designed for you and why that's important? By establishing goals that are designed and tailored for you and following these simple steps you too can increase your percentage of *accomplished* goals vs. *established* goals.

Stay Focused/Avoid Excuses. Keep your eyes focused on your target in life. You cannot reach a destination by looking back where you came from. When times get rough, and they will, you must keep your eyes focused on your goal. My prayer every morning is that I keep my eyes focused on the Lord, never deviating, never swaying. If along the way, you make a mistake, and you will, remember this: A mistake is nothing more than the beginning of learning how to do something right. Learn from it and go on.

True Prosperity

In previous talks with other doctors, I would tell them to keep their eyes focused on the goals they had established before them. I would often use an analogy of a successful doctor vs. an unsuccessful doctor with success being defined in office visits. When the unsuccessful doctor is ridiculed for trying to better him or herself, it goes directly to the part of the brain that causes the goals to become blurry and eventually focus is lost. Breaking out of a mold is too hard to this individual at the price of losing communion with the peers he or she has established. On the other hand, the successful person would not allow this sort of thing to distract her. She would let it roll off like water on ducks feathers. Remember the duck theory? Don't allow others to rain on your parade. Subscribe to the duck theory and stay focused. It's your life. Live it the way God intended you to.

I hear too many people say they don't have the time to establish goals. This is probably the biggest excuse of all, but I believe the real problem is much deeper than that. You see we can find time for the things we feel are important. Have you ever taken a look at yourself or someone else prior to taking a vacation? The amount of work that is put out is more than double that of an ordinary day. Why? Because we believe that we must take care of or do the work we would have normally done while at home prior to leaving. We make the time. Wouldn't it be wonderful if we worked like this without a vacation to motivate us?

So if time isn't it, what is? My opinion is it's fear. Fear of failure. Fear of committing to something and falling short in front of others. Zig Ziglar said it so well when he described fear

The Boat Without a Sail

as "False Evidence Appearing Real." Fear makes the wolf bigger than he is.

You will never accomplish the things you desire to in life without facing your fears head on. If your fear is what will others say, face it by telling them your goals. Let me warn you however, there are those goals you tell and those you don't. For instance, losing weight would be one you should tell. Someone can then hold you accountable. If you fail, pick yourself up and try again. On the other hand, goals that involve a personal relationship with your spouse (family oriented) or with your relationship with God (spiritually oriented) may be ones you keep to yourself and share with only one that you can trust or not at all. Since we are all descendants of Adam, we all lack in many areas and we all need help. Keep good company. If you are going to strive to make your life count for something, associate with those that believe and feel as you do. Don't subject yourself to the *outhouse syndrome*. I know what you're thinking. What's the outhouse syndrome? Simply this, you may not be an outhouse, but if you sit in one long enough you will begin to smell like one. Like it or not. Likewise, if you associate with negative people long enough you *will* soak up negativity. No ifs, ands or buts about it! Organize your time, face your fears and avoid the outhouse syndrome. By doing so, you will find that you not only have the time, you can do it!

Let me summarize this chapter for you. You must have goals. The first and most important thing you can do with your life is to give yourself totally to the Lord. Once you have done that, realize that all of us must always work to be better fathers, mothers, husbands, wives, bosses, Christians, businessmen, businesswomen, etc. Based on that fact, we must

True Prosperity

have a specific goal or achieving point in mind to strive for. Although we will never be perfect, establishing and pursuing new goals in life brings the happiness that so many people are looking for everyday.

So many are looking for happiness in all the wrong places. Look within. God can give you joy. Only you can give yourself happiness. Happiness begins with a purpose and goal to strive for. It's been said that one of the most devastating things you can do with your life is to wake up one day and realize that you are not all that you can be because you failed to try. It's your responsibility.

The Boat Without a Sail

8
Charting Your Course

Now that you have learned how to sail in life and to rely on God when you are in *irons*, you must begin charting your course for tomorrow. If I asked you to write down the goals you had in life at the beginning of this book, what would they have been? Where were you headed if your goals in life depended on it? Did they include the immediate as well as the future? At this point, are they somewhat different than before?

For most, our life is not headed in the direction we would like it to. I know when I was first taught about goals, I got to the point that I despised hearing about them much less establishing one. Goals for this. Goals for that. I was told to write them down daily and evaluate what I did the day before that brought me closer to my target—everyday! Now I realize that as important as goals are, (even daily ones) we must chart the course of life in a way we can remain motivated and avoid burnout. Just as you can become frustrated with a goal that is unattainable, you can react the same by overdoing it. Very few, if any, can honestly establish daily goals and follow the criteria we set forth in the previous chapter, including this one, without suffering burnout and giving up.

I consider myself a relatively motivated person that attempts to walk the walk as well as talk the talk. I have found it very difficult to establish and maintain daily goals. Beginning is easy. Finishing is another story. Daily *to-do lists* or *accomplishment lists*

True Prosperity

are another story. Each day I write down the things that I need to accomplish the following day. As they are completed, I check them off approaching each one in order. Do I always accomplish all of the items I wrote down for that day? Absolutely not! Some may remain for several days until completion for one reason or another.

The point is that they remain until I have completed them. It's easy to tell you to write down what you want to do each day. I could suggest that you write your day's accomplishments. But how realistic is that? You may do that for several days or weeks but how about a year from now? Statistically few, if any, would continue that type of goal setting on a daily basis.

Don't misunderstand me. I am not saying daily goals are unnecessary. What I am saying is that you must be realistic in your actions. I told you in the beginning that I was not interested in just motivating you, but rather giving you ways to make a real lasting change in your life. In order to do so, we must use principles that are easy to adhere to although the goal itself may be difficult. Otherwise we will give up when, in all actuality, the goal we were headed for was blocked only by the steps we took to get there.

Let's take a close look at how to establish the course you want your life headed on. Remember, the road you follow is in your hands.

You Must Be Honest With Yourself. Honesty is the best policy. If you are headed west, you can believe you are headed south indefinitely and it will not change your direction. In fact, what it will do is cause you to be more determined, blinded and defiant to the truth causing you to head further

Charting Your Course

and further toward the wrong destination. Be honest with yourself about the direction your life is headed and whether you will do what it takes to change it. Also be honest about the goals you establish.

We discussed being sure your goals were tailored for you. It is equally important, however, to be sure you are willing to follow them through. You can establish a goal with all the criteria necessary to follow it through and fail based on your mind set at the time.

I realize we have used weight loss as an example more than once, but I do so because it is easy for most to relate to. You have often seen people begin diets and end them before they were completed. Provided these goals were established correctly and they were put to the test we have outlined, it would become obvious that the individual didn't have the mindset to complete it.

Goals take change just as life does. Should you decide today that you are going to chart a new course for your life, you must be willing to change. It may be a change in your mind set, surroundings or some type of action, but you will have to change. If change is not in your vocabulary, then accomplishing a goal that requires it will not be part of your life. Just mentioning the word change frightens people. According to Michael O'Neal the strategy for successful change takes the following main steps:
    1. When you change your thinking, you change your beliefs.
    2. When you change your beliefs, you change your expectations.

3. When your expectations change, your attitude will change.
4. When you change your attitude, you change your behavior.
5. When you change your behavior, you change your performance.
6. When you change your performance, you change your life.

He further states that we often make two bad mistakes:
1. We wait for God to change our circumstances.
2. We wait for our circumstances to change our behavior.

All of us have desired results in our lives. Goals we want accomplished. Things we wish to attain. Changes we wish to make. None of these, however, are attainable without changing ourselves.

So be honest with yourself about your goals and realize you must be willing to change. Then and only then will you attain truly desired results in your life.

Be Specific. When deciding where you want your life to be, a vague description will not bring you any closer to that destination. You must be specific concerning your goals. "I want to own my own business in five years" is not a specific goal. You will be no closer to reaching it than if you said nothing at all.

As you map out your life, think of the bottom line. In other words, delete all the "fluff" and narrow in on precisely what you want. You can do so by realizing the end result of your goal.

Charting Your Course

Let's take several examples of this so that you may see what it is I am trying to relate to you.

Should you have a family goal to change your life by being a better spouse. What is the end result of that goal? In other words, what exactly are you trying to improve? Is it patience? Anger? Helping around the house? Maybe it's being a better listener. Regardless of what it is, you must define it if you are going to re-route your life.

A specific goal in this area may be "I want be a better spouse by learning to listen better and having more patience with my mate." Now you can work on those areas and develop specific action steps to do them. Although a realistic time period should be established, with goals that involve change from within do not become discouraged should you not make your deadline. Real change takes place gradually, never suddenly.

Another example may involve your spiritual life. People set goals to read their Bible more often. Although there is nothing wrong with that goal, something is missing. You need to define the goal more specifically in detail. A more specific goal would be, I will read my Bible daily beginning [date]. Or I will read the entire Bible in one year, reading a specific amount daily. Now you have not only defined what it is you want to do, but exactly what you are trying to accomplish. Get the picture?

Being specific in your goal setting will not only allow you to establish goals that are realistically attainable, but also place you on the path you have chosen for your life.

I am a firm believer that there is no such thing as luck with few exceptions (i.e. lottery, etc.). People who have begun with nothing and ended with something had a specific vision of what they wanted and made sacrifices as well as changes. Sam

True Prosperity

Walton didn't decide one day that he would just open up a store and see what would happened. His vision and goal was specific. He desired to provide America with a discount center that under one roof people could find the best prices with the best service. He didn't waiver. He was specific in his desires and honest with himself about the goals he set out to accomplish.

Have you had difficulty in accomplishing your goals? If so, I urge you to evaluate how specific they are. Odds are you will find that they need some fine-tuning. Until you know specifically what you want, you cannot lay out a plan to attain it, and with no plan there's no hope for a goal becoming a reality. It will remain a dream, indefinitely.

Establish Short and Long Term Goals. As you write down goals for your life, it is imperative that you chart them out both short and long term. Most individuals will establish long term goals without looking at the short term as well. That's like learning to run before learning to walk! Long term goals are those goals that are established for the long-term. In order to reach these goals we must have *stepping-stones*. These stepping-stones are known as short-term goals. True you can have short-term goals with no long-term outlook, but somewhere down the line you will be facing a black wall for tomorrow.

Let's say you establish a financial goal to accumulate a specific amount of money. But your real underlying interest is in becoming debt free.

Although your short term goal of accumulating certain assets is important toward becoming debt free, years later you could find yourself in the same situation you are in when you started without laying out your goals and action steps on a long term

Charting Your Course

basis.

By looking far enough ahead, you can lay out a plan including the obstacles that may arise along the way. Without looking far enough ahead, chance and circumstance will determine where you go. Short-term goals on the other hand enable you to attain your long-term goals, and having goals in general increase efficiency and effectiveness, making it easier for you to make decisions.

Now that we have discussed the reasons for goals as well as how to establish them, I want to give you the opportunity to establish your own. On the following page, take the next few minutes to establish your short and long term goals in life. Use the following summary to work by as you chart out a course for your life.

No one can make you do this part. It's up to you and you alone. Just remember that you chose to make the initiative by reading this book. If you don't follow through, you're establishing the goal (both short and long term) of remaining where you are at in life with chance and circumstance being your navigator.

Goal Setting Summary

- Determine if your goals are desired for you by asking the three following questions (Refer to Chapter 7 of this section if necessary for a better understanding of those questions):
    1. Does this goal inflict pain on anyone?

True Prosperity

      2. Will my goals cause me to turn my back on God by placing their accomplishments and their attainment higher than he places on my priority list?
      3. Does praying about those goals cause an "uneasiness" within my spirit?

- Look at yourself from the outside in
- Stay focused/Avoid excuses
- Be honest with yourself about your goals
- Be specific

My Short Term Goals

Charting Your Course

My Long Term Goals

   Should you follow the above criteria and have a *yes* answer to the above questions, you are well on your way to the success in life you desire. No one said it was going to be easy. As the old saying goes "Nothing worthwhile ever is." There should be no argument that God is in charge of our ultimate destiny. We, however, have a choice of which path we follow in this life. Just as you would prepare a map for a vacation to somewhere you have never traveled, so also should you prepare your real map for life?

True Prosperity

Hopefully by now you can see that success means so much more than money. As a matter of fact, money is only one facet of being successful. Truly successful people have much more than financial freedom. Truly successful people have relationships, loving relationships. If I were to draw a diagram of what success actually is, I believe it would look somewhat like a cross section of an onion with the nucleus being made up of the three Rs (Relationships with God, Family and Friends).

Loving Relationships = Success

Charting Your Course

There are probably many of you reading this book that are caught somewhere between surrendering to God and believing in God. Be assured there's quite a difference. Let me explain.

Years ago there were a variety of scandals that took place throughout the Christian community. I recall a specific one that literally shocked the strongest believers. A man who appeared dedicated to God, his family and his ministry fell from grace. Not once, but twice. I believe the thing that shocked everyone the most was his superficial lifestyle, background, and outspoken adversity toward the very thing he fell from.

Not long after that incident I came to know of several people who literally threw away their Bibles and haven't been to church since. I found that hard to swallow but, as hard as it was, it was true. So what's the point? These individuals were hurt and found it hard to forgive, right? That's partially true, but the real truth comes in what I spoke of earlier. Believing in something is an act that anyone can do by simply expressing words. A relationship is totally different. Unfortunately, the people I spoke of before were worshipping a man, not God.

Although there are no statistics or scientific barometer to measure success in people, I have yet to see true happiness in a person who doesn't have at least one loving relationship in life. I told you in previous chapters about the sign I have on the door of my office that reads, "I don't know the secret to success, but I do know the secret to failure—trying to please everyone!" This sign, although entertaining and true to a certain point, doesn't express the total truth. That's because the secret to success is being unveiled for you and all that seek to find it. Loving relationships beginning with the highest source are the key to the success this world is searching for.

True Prosperity

Anger often blocks us from enjoying these relationships. As a story goes, there was a little boy with a bad temper. His father gave him a bag of nails. He told the boy to hammer a nail in the back fence whenever he lost his temper.

The first day the boy had driven 37 nails into the fence. Each successive day, however, he nailed fewer nails. He discovered it was easier to hold his temper than to drive those nails into the fence.

Finally the day came when the boy didn't lose his temper at all. When He told his father about it, the father suggested that the boy now pull out one nail for each day that he was able to hold his temper. The days passed and the young boy was finally able to tell his father that all the nails were gone.

The father took his son by the hand and led him to the fence. He said, "You have done well, my son, but look at the holes in the fence. The fence will never be the same.

"When you say things in anger, they leave a scar just like this one. You can put a knife in a man and draw it out. It won't matter how many times you say *I'm sorry*, the wound is still there. A verbal wound is as bad as a physical one."

Will a relationship with God and family bring you money? Not necessarily. But my question is, Will money without a relationship with God and family bring you happiness? And if you answer that question as I believe you will, I could go one step further. Can you have true fulfilling success in life without happiness? That joy, happiness and fulfillment can motivate even the least motivated to shoot for the stars. After all what is financial success without someone to share it with? Many fail to realize that having a loving relationship with God through Christ is the key to success. Sure many go to church. More say

Charting Your Course

they believe. A relationship, however, is an intimate communion between you and God, your family and your friends. Just as you speak to those around you, so also can you speak to God. Look to Him as your source for everything. He is the best advisor for all life's questions you will ever have. With Him as the captain of your ship, charting your course in life will be much easier not to mention a whole lot more enjoyable.

Likewise, friends are a very rare jewel indeed. They make you smile and encourage you to succeed. They lend an ear. They share your dreams. They share a word of praise, and they always want to open their hearts to you. Show your friends how much you care about them.

9
Reaching Your Destination

As you now realize, achieving personal success in life is much more than driving a nice car and enjoying the materialistic things of life. If you have read each chapter thoroughly, it should now become evident to you that we have outlined the basic anatomy of the *how-tos* of attaining success in your life. Within this section, we have explained the definition of goals, their basic importance, why we should have them and how to establish them correctly. Now let's take a close look at how establishing your road map in life leads to reaching your destination with a simple explanation.

Most of us have taken a vacation. Traveling can be exciting provided it's well planned. Wherever you travel, however, if you don't plan properly a vacation can turn into nothing less than a nightmare. No one likes to waste time, especially on your vacation. Without a plan you'll find yourself wandering around like a pet in the wild. You may get there eventually, but you'll be frustrated, physically, mentally and emotionally exhausted, ready to collapse.

It's somewhat like the boat without a sail. You've got the boat and water, but you are missing the main ingredient: The winds that push you along! Now let's say you have that wind, you are well prepared and your course is well charted. Your trip goes well. It's on schedule with some unforeseen obstacles, but for the most part, you planned well!

True Prosperity

Finally, you reach your destination. It's a place you have wanted to go all of your life, perhaps a tropical island. When you get there, it's as beautiful as you expected. Your two-week adventure leads you on a journey that you will never forget.

Eventually you realize that you only have one day left in this paradise. You have planned for as long as you can remember and in 24 hours it's all over. Suddenly you feel somewhat sick and depressed. You have reached the destination you've always dreamed of and it's all over. You return home with pictures, stories and memories that last forever, but something is missing. What is it? The answer is simple. It's the excitement that comes with following a proper course in life, mapped out and planned.

The realization that a goal—money, a house, a car, etc.—has been attained brings with it a sense of disappointment at the same time. What now? Another goal? Most people who attain the success in life they once desired are left unfulfilled. They look around and wonder, Is this it? Is this all life has to offer? I have known people that have come from nothing and climbed their way up the ladder of life only to find unhappiness at the top.

Many star athletes find themselves depressed and on drugs. Once playing professionally was all that mattered. No one could have convinced them that the professional status they strive for wouldn't bring the success and happiness they desired. You have heard stories all of your life of "successful" people that died unhappy, unfulfilled and depressed.

Howard Hughes, one of the wealthiest men of our time, died this way. There are people who thought that if they could just get their hands on a million dollars everything would be okay.

Reaching Your Destination

Yet we read about those who win the lottery that are unfulfilled. They wish they had never played the game much less won the money.

So what am I saying? Forget dreaming and establishing goals because if you get there you will not be happy anyway? Of course not! I am saying that you need to understand the basic anatomy of success and happiness.

According to Webster's dictionary, success is defined as follows:

> 1. result; outcome 2. a favorable or satisfactory outcome or result 3. the gaining of wealth, fame, rank, etc. 4. a successful person or thing.

It goes on to describe such synonyms of success as achievement, luck, consummation, prosperity, and victory. Successful on the other hand is defined as follows:

> 1. coming about, taking place, or turning out to be as was hoped for; having a favorable result; as, a successful mission 2. achieving or having achieved success; specifically, having gained wealth, fame, rank, etc.

Synonyms listed for successful are: fortunate, prosperous, lucky, and effectual.

In the above definitions we see that being successful in worldly terms is merely achieving the success defined for us by others. Although having financial success is part of the overall picture, money does not define being successful. If it were, we wouldn't see so many unhappy rich people in the media everyday. If we are to be successful by striving for our goals, what exactly do we do once we achieve them? Remember our tropical

True Prosperity

vacation that we looked forward to all our lives? We planned and set savings goals long before we boarded the plane. While on the flight if we thought reaching our goal wouldn't bring total fulfillment we would obviously be disappointed. No one specific goal, achievement or attainment will make you fulfilled or happy. Success in life is much more than that. It carries with it a sense of peace about today and an excitement about what tomorrow holds.

To be satisfied as you attain your goal requires maintaining perspective. It is not enough to set and then achieve your goals. One needs to learn how to live once you've reached it. Here are five strategies for living your goal.

Five Strategies for Living Your Goal

1. Realize What Success Actually Is

By realizing what success actually is, we can prevent many of the downfalls that accompany it. Striving for the goals in life that lead to the success you desire is just a small part of what it takes to remain at the top. The rewards you have and continue to reap in life are due more to your mindset than anything else. If then, we are influenced by what affects our minds, we must be particular about who we associate with. The few people that experience true personal success will tell you that. Although they have a love for mankind, they are leery about who they spend their time with.

Zig Ziglar once said, "You are what you are and where you are because of what goes into your mind." How true that statement is. I believe I described it best as the *outhouse syndrome*. The idea being you may not be one, but if you hang

Reaching Your Destination

out long enough in one you may begin to smell like an outhouse.

Even fewer who reach the top remain successful. Why? It's simple. They have unrealistic expectations. They simply don't know what success really is. You must realize that success does not bring happiness. You are ultimately responsible for your own happiness. True success brings with it a sense of personal accomplishment and satisfaction that ultimately leads to confidence in ourselves. Self-confidence is important in the overall picture of happiness.

Realize that reaching the top does not solve all of life's problems. What we have today can be taken away tomorrow. Reminding ourselves of this keeps us humble.

Remember where you were when you set your goal and how far you've come. And understand that you will remain you regardless of what you accomplish or possess. That's the first key to maintaining what you spend a great deal of your life attaining.

2. Set New Goals

Goals again? You bet! A life without goals is like a morning without orange juice or a day without sunshine? Well it doesn't change when you accomplish lifetime dreams. Unless of course, your life is over. You must always look for ways to better yourself in all aspects of your life.

To say that you don't need to do so is arrogance and with arrogance breeds pride. Allow me to tell you something profound. You never will be perfect. Surprised? We all need to change and change is constant, never ending. Granted, your goals may change, but the importance of having them doesn't.

True Prosperity

Besides no one just coasts through life. You either continue to grow or you stagnate and die. It is a simple choice.

3. Look for Advice in All the Right Places

Sounds like a song doesn't it? For the sake of this chapter, let's call it the song of life. In many ways, we discussed this in the first strategy when we spoke of choosing your company well. I feel, however, that the company you choose and the advice you seek are two separate and entirely different things. No matter how good the company is that I keep I am not inclined to seek advice from all of them, quite the opposite as a matter of fact. Seek advice from people who are successful in the areas you are interested in. More than that, be sure they share your similar beliefs in the area.

For instance, let's say you're thinking about getting into the rental real estate market on a conservative basis. You have decided to stay with single family homes with the following qualifications:

1. 3 bedroom/2 bath
2. House on a slab
3. Quality neighborhood with little crime

You want to begin slowly with only one. Should it prove to be successful, you may look at another. You set out to talk with someone that is successful in the real estate market. You are referred to a man that owns an army of real estate from homes to commercial buildings. Great! What a better person to talk to right? Well, maybe. Suppose this person tells you that the only way to get into real estate is head first. "Just jump in and don't look back," he says. He tells you that he has five homes for sale now that are all rented and he will make you the deal of a

Reaching Your Destination

lifetime.

You look at what he has and realize that only one of the homes meet your criteria and it's not exactly what you wanted. The man is pushy and eventually writes you off as someone that is all talk and no action. Is this person someone for you to seek advice from? He is in the business and successful, but his beliefs of how to get there are totally different than yours? So do you give in saying I'll do it his way, or do you seek someone that's more compatible with your way of thinking?

I believe the choice is obvious. As good as the stock market has been to certain people, it has also been not so good to others. That's why everyone is different in his or her initial approach. The same is true of real estate or any other venture in life. Don't trust advice from just anyone and be sure you can back it up with sound biblical economics. If not, you may want to find someone else.

4. Keep Hope By Remaining Spiritually Focused
Sometime ago I was watching a famous radio/television show host being interviewed on NBC's Dateline. He described his life and all of the ups and downs accompanying it. He once achieved success on his terms and later fell from the ladder. He had been married to four different women and was presently single. When asked about his life and the financial success he now enjoys, he commented that no woman could ever take the place of the camera. He went on to say that his biggest fear in life was death. Having lived through a heart attack, he hated that he didn't see a tunnel of light or any other sign of the hereafter. He was therefore sure that this life was all there was. "This is it," he said.

True Prosperity

Watching that program, I wondered how this man defined success and whether he believed he had attained all life had to offer him. I can't imagine going through life believing that death is ultimate and there is no hereafter. How can you enjoy success or for that matter, even attain it without being spiritually focused? By humbling ourselves to a greater authority, we can keep things in perspective, as they should be. If we allow our spiritual eyes to wander, regardless of our beliefs, we will never enjoy the true joy, peace and happiness life has to offer. Being prepared for death does create a peace within that fills a void, an emptiness and blackness. It's what I refer to as the *black hole*. No matter what you attain, accomplish or become you will never have true peace, joy and happiness until you fill the black hole of your soul. Religion will not do it. Philosophy will not do it. False doctrine will not do it.

John 3:16 sums it all up, "For God so loved the world that he gave his one and only Son, that whoever believes in him shall not perish, but have everlasting life." He came that you may have life and have it more abundantly. Keep focused. Keep your faith, and hope will come naturally.

5. Avoid Failure at all cost

At all cost! That's pretty tough isn't it? Yes, it is. But if you understand what success is and what the consequences of failure are, you will soon realize that avoiding failure is the only way to go.

Stated another way, play to win! Life is tough; there is no question about it. But I don't believe it's too tough for us to succeed in. If that were the case we would be basically saying that God created us and placed us on this earth to fail because

Reaching Your Destination

success was not possible! That obviously doesn't hold water.

A word of caution is needed here. Success in individual areas (i.e. spiritual, family) should not be sacrificed to avoid failure in other areas. When I say to avoid failure at all cost, I am speaking of failing at life, failing at the success you desire for yourself to include these things. We have already discussed their importance. You must realize you cannot succeed without them, to sacrifice them would not be avoiding failure.

Having always been taught I now teach my children: when you play a game, you play to win. Does this mean you should cheat, hurt others or violate sound biblical principals to do so? Absolutely not! What it does mean is that you should be focused on your goal, be prepared and persevere until the end regardless of the outcome. Keeping your eyes on the goal means focusing on your God and your family while you are pursuing your goals. Being prepared means you should look at all of your obstacles and be prepared for all that may come your way. And persevering—well, it means just that—never, ever quit.

Let's now take a closer look at the key obstacles that cause failure in people today. There are many mountains to climb on your way to attaining your success; however, these five seem to always reveal themselves regardless of the goal pursued.

Five Keys to Avoiding Failure

1. Uncontrollable Frustration

Face it. No matter who you are and what your lifestyle is, you will sooner or later be frustrated in some form or another. When pursuing success by establishing goals and attempting

True Prosperity

to balance your life, you will encounter frustration. The closer you get to your goal and the more successful you become the more important it is that you learn how to handle frustration. It goes hand in hand with success, especially in the area of finances.

The more money you have the more you will have to learn to control frustration. I don't know of one person that has accumulated wealth that hasn't encountered it! Not one! Frustration can kill a dream, which in turn kills goals, which in turn causes failure in people.

Every success story in life contains mounds and mounds of frustration. Things don't go right. Goals aren't met on time. Obstacles arise that you never expected. Do you think Donald Trump built his financial empire without frustration? As a matter of fact, he is probably frustrated now trying to keep it!

You show me a successful person and I'll show you someone who can confront and handle frustration. You may think you're broke because you're frustrated, but you have it backwards my friend. People get paid well for coping with stress and frustration. All successful people realize that you must dig through the frustration before you can find success. Success is the diamond in the rough and the rough is the frustration. Benjamin Disraeli once wrote, "Little things affect little minds." That goes well in understanding frustration.

If we realize that we shouldn't worry about the little things in life, and it's all little things, then we can realize we shouldn't let it affect us. Frustration teaches us as we move along the road of life towards success. With each obstacle there is frustration. With each frustrating moment there is a learning experience and a chance to regroup. If I were asked what the key to failure

Reaching Your Destination

was in one word, it would be frustration. The key to success? Handling it.

2. Avoiding Rejection
I spoke in an earlier chapter about Colonel Sanders and his endurance in receiving 1,000 noes before hearing the sought after yes. That's just one of the many ways rejection will be your companion on the path to success.

Speaking of rejection reminds me of when I was a recent graduate with high ambitions of establishing a practice. My vision was establishing a multi-doctor facility that would project a professional image on my chosen profession. This had not been done thus far, at least not in my part of the country. Little did I know that my vision was smaller than the attained dream would become! Although I attained a goal beyond my expectations, rejection filled the air throughout my journey in life. Here goes another profound statement. It still does!

Rejection is part of life if you are going to strive for anything outside of the norm. I was told all along that I would fail. "You must be crazy if you think you're going to create a practice like that in this town." "Don't try it Dallas, you'll regret it." Or consider this one, "If you want to live your life in debt and constantly scrape by, just go through with what you're doing. I would advise you to get a job and work like everybody else!"

I never quite figured that one out. I guess that person believed if I established my own business I wouldn't work. Regardless, the point is rejection is a black cloud that will follow you around throughout your goal setting life. You can look at it as a dark cloud raining on your parade or you can view it as the storm before the sunshine. If you see it as the latter, you will

True Prosperity

learn to look past the rejection to the clear sky ahead. Rejection builds character and character is what is left after all of the noes are gone.

If you were told you could do anything and would not be rejected, what would you do? Would you try things that you would not have otherwise? Inventions would be accepted, job applications accepted, ideas accepted, business loan applications accepted, requests accepted and on the list could go. Why not view your journey and attained success the same way? All someone can do is say no and noes have kept good company. Show me a successful person in life and I will show you someone who faces rejection head-on, over and over and over and—well, you get the picture.

3. Avoiding Financial Pressure

This may sound like a no-brainer, but you would be surprised at the number of people who believe when you "make it" your financial worries are over. Hogwash! If you choose to attain the success you desire in your life and finances are part of it, get ready!

During my growth phase in business, I can recall financial pressure above all things, tremendous financial pressure. Bills due, payroll due, rent due, notes overdue, the pressure was enormous. We covered finances in some detail before. I explained to you that no other area can penetrate your life like financial pressure.

In the upcoming chapter we will discuss how to live beyond financial pressure. You do not have to become a slave to it. After working through the mistakes I made during my growth phase, I encountered financial pressure, but to a much lesser extent. I learned to give it to God and do all I can humanly do. I worried less and eventually put it behind me altogether.

Do I avoid financial pressure? No! I face it, handle it, and attempt to circumvent it as much as possible by looking ahead on a regular basis. God will lead you, but you can't sit back and just wait for a miracle. Financial pressure, if avoided, can lead to financial devastation. Financial pressure if confronted and handled wrongly can lead to the worse kind of destruction, your life. Don't avoid financial pressure. Realize it's part of the wheel of success. A piece of the overall puzzle we all must confront.

4. Complacency
It goes without saying that you can't reach the pinnacle of success by being complacent—No argument there. Why then is it that so many those attaining success believe they can become complacent once they've achieved it? People reach a desired level of success only to fall long and hard because of something avoidable. That something is mental laziness, also known as complacency.

There's nothing wrong with being happy with your accomplishments. There's nothing wrong with enjoying some of the benefits. There is something terribly wrong with becoming complacent and not being all that got you to where you are today. The power of the mouth that accompanies complacency causes tremendous devastation. You utter the words, "I've made it. I think I can stop trying and start enjoying, I deserve it." Just be ready for a fall. Luke 18:14b reads, "For everyone who exalts himself will be humbled, and he who humbles himself will be exalted."

True Prosperity

Proverbs happens to be one of my favorite books of the Bible. Solomon specifically discusses being aware of the words we speak from our lips. He spends time on laziness too. These two subjects I believe, are of utmost importance when discussing complacency and reaching our desired destination in life. "Do not love to sleep or you will grow poor; stay awake and you will have food to spare" (Proverbs 20:13). I don't know about you, but that seems self-explanatory to me!

Of these six things the Lord hates, a proud look is one of them (cf. Proverbs 6:16-17). Don't become a victim of complacency and don't allow your mouth to become your enemy. Remember, money may talk, but wealth whispers.

5. Greed

In Section 2 of this book, we discussed ten financial principals to live by. The fifth principle, if followed properly, would prevent this stage from ever occurring.

Years ago Burt Reynolds starred in a film with Dom DeLuise entitled *The End*. It depicted a man portrayed by Burt Reynolds that wanted to end his life and tried various ways to commit suicide. All failed and then the finale came. He decided to drown himself. He swam a long distance and dove deep as he attempted to end his life. Then suddenly he came up gasping for air determined to live. As he fought for his life swimming toward shore he began promising God to tithe with his money. He started with 80%! As he got closer to the shore the percentages fell. Soon he saw that he was going to make it. The percentage went to, and I'm guessing, somewhere around 10%. He finally told the Lord to either take it or leave it; that's his final offer!

Reaching Your Destination

Although humorous, this reflects life much as it is today. We want to give when we are asking for help; however, we feel we can discontinue when times are good and we don't need the help anymore. Nothing could be further from the truth. Greed can kill even the best of people. It is the center of every backstabbing, cutthroat transaction in this world today. "What's in it for me?" is one of the most common asked questions and could be coined as the slogan of this decade.

Think about it. What would happen to this world if there were no greed? Everyone would be as interested in everyone else as they were themselves. The *in it for me* philosophy would be history and the thought of how different things would be is mind-boggling.

So what does this have to do with reaching your destination in life? Everything! If you reach your desired level of success with greed, it won't be what you desired at all. It's false success and the only way to stay there would be by lying and cheating. Not my idea of being successful. On the other hand, if you reach that level as we have outlined in this book, you should realize that greed will take away everything you achieved in a fraction of time.

I have personally witnessed people, truly successful people, allow greed to take over and end up lower than where they originally started in life. The sad part about it is that greed is like a cancer. Once you allow it to take hold, it eats at you until there's nothing left. The good thing about it is there is a proven prevention: Give, give and give some more. Following these simple rules and understanding the five keys to failure will allow you to avoid the failures that face all as you reach these destinations in life.

True Prosperity

Now that we have outlined the way to reach success in life and what to do when it has been attained, it's important we discuss what comes next. True, we talked about strategies to live by when gaining success and keys to avoid failing, but how about living in general. How do you live the successful life successfully?

During this next section, we will cover living the successful life with a look at various attributes and guidelines to live by that I believe you will find entertaining and informative. That along with this chapter will form the rock-solid foundation whereupon fruit-bearing success can grow. Not only in your life but in others also as they follow in your example.

Reaching Your Destination

Section Four

Living the Successful Life

To Think of Success is a dream.
To prepare for success is a plan.
To strive for success takes action.
To live successfully you must believe.
To believe makes living successfully a reality.

Do not let this Book of the Law depart from your mouth; meditate on it day and night, so that you may be careful to do everything written in it. Then you will be prosperous and successful.
—Joshua 1:8

10
Living Beyond Financial Slavery

Financial slavery is a reality in the United States and throughout the world today. People from all walks of life are consumed with debt and are slaves to their lenders. Debt has become easy. Young people are now leaving college to begin their careers with five and six figure loans. Our nation has undergone a transformation that was not intended by our founding fathers. Hard work and success are synonymous terms. Biblical laws of prosperity require us to work hard if we want to prosper.

The Bible says in II Thessalonians 3:10, "If a man will not work, he shall not eat." As obvious as this sounds, the work ethic and service in this country have withered away with time. People want something for nothing and are determined to have their share of the American dream without working for it.

Get rich quick schemes fill the air around us. Commercials air with people promising wealth without work. In other words, they promote going from step one to step ten while bypassing steps two through nine. More emphasis is being placed on having fun, being free and looking out for "number one." Many people have lived by this philosophy since they were born, but times are changing. For every action there is an equal and opposite reaction. The reaction is being seen throughout this country.

True Prosperity

The basic truth of II Thessalonians 3:10 has been ignored by bureaucrats responsible for a top heavy, illiquid government. Welfare has become a way of life rather than a way back to work. Our government, founded on basic Judeo-Christian concepts, has been replaced by human greed. Rather than elected officials representing the people, they represent the special interest groups that bought them the office. Many judges in this country are bought off by large corporations expecting rulings in their favor should future litigation occur.

The United States is now paying the price for its ignorance. We have people that have never worked a day in their lives. Yet they live better than many hard working Americans. Governmental handouts rather than hard work have erased the poverty level. My hat is off to those who earn their way out of poverty. They deserve to enjoy the fruits of their labor. The system was designed for those individuals that could not work for legitimate reasons. Many people don't work and wouldn't work if you gave them a job.

If success is in our vocabulary, we need to eliminate get rich quick schemes and handouts to those that do not want to work. The biblical laws of prosperity are self-explanatory when it comes to success and prosperity. "Go to the ant, thou sluggard; consider her ways, and be wise: Which having no guide, overseer, or ruler, providith her meat in the summer, and gatherith her food in the harvest" (Proverbs 6:6-9). Laziness and success are completely opposite. Laziness produces poverty. Hard work produces success. People no longer have an initiative to become entrepreneurial and start a business. Primarily this is due to the government penalizing hard working Americans and rewarding lazy ones.

Living Beyond Financial Slavery

I read a letter once by a gentleman complaining of the tax code in this country. It was obvious that this individual was part of the "give me, I deserve it" crowd. When explaining the way he believes the tax law should be, he wrote, "I believe the tax rate should be 50% of everything earned to $500,000, 70% of everything earned between $500,000 and $1,000,000 and 90% of everything earned above $1,000,000."

Granted these income levels represent a fraction of this nation's population, but is it fair to tax at this rate if someone works hard and earns it honestly? I often wondered if this individual would approve of these tax laws if he won the lottery. Odds are he would adamantly object.

The entrepreneurial spirit has made America what it is today. Now jobs, incentives, better incomes, etc., are all produced because of someone's vision. Would you want a blind person to lead you across a busy intersection? No, you would want someone with vision. This country, however, is being led by blind people with no vision penalizing the producers and rewarding the non-producers.

Can this all change? I believe it can. I have hope for our country and I think that if we go back to the original biblical concepts we were founded on we can succeed. But not without learning several important issues to avoid and living beyond the financial slavery trap. The first five of these guidelines are the basic financial foundations laid down by Solomon in the book of Proverbs so that we may experience financial freedom. They are listed below for your reference. If you are going to achieve success and not become a victim of financial slavery, I believe this groundwork is the basic foundation to begin working from.

True Prosperity

Then and only then can we enjoy success as God intended it to be.

Guidelines for Avoiding Financial Slavery

1. Keep Good Records
Proverbs 27:23-24a says, "Be sure to know the condition of your flocks, give careful attention to your herds; for riches do not endure forever." Put in another way, riches can disappear fast, so watch your business interest closely. You need to know where you are in order to know where you are going. The importance of keeping good records cannot be stressed enough.

Proverbs 23:23 tells us to get the facts at any price. Many people have checkbooks that are nothing less than a disaster. They couldn't find a receipt or cancelled check if they had to. Don't fall short of financial freedom because your records are not up to par. Make keeping good records part of your overall financial plan. With today's computer technology and software programs you have no excuse for not having your financial records up to date and accurate.

2. Plan your spending
How do you spell relief? R-O-L-A-I-D-S? Well for some maybe, but for those of us that wish to have financial relief it's spelled B-U-D-G-E-T. Having a spending plan or budget to adhere to is imperative in your overall plan for financial freedom. Impulse buying is literally eating away at our society by creating wants through the use of advertising. To give you an example, my son (8 years old at the time of this story) came to me some

Living Beyond Financial Slavery

time ago asking me for my credit card after watching a commercial! He not only wanted it; he was some kind of upset for not receiving it. He told me that a commercial was on TV that was offering something he wanted and he would never have the chance to buy it again.

That's the problem with our society. You must buy now or you will never have the same opportunity. The sales pitches that are given completely astound me. "Only 152 easy payments...no payments until January the year after next!" I don't know about you, but I never met an easy payment plan in my entire life.

Proverbs 21:5 says, "Plans of the diligent lead to profit as surely as haste leads to poverty." Look at verse 20b, "But a foolish man devours all he has." The Good News Version is even more direct in it's writing, "Stupid people spend their money as fast as they get it."

In chapter six I explain in describing a financial principle the importance of living by a budget. Another principle in this chapter explains how you should never make a business decision under pressure.

It is wise to plan your spending regardless of how much money you have. The most financially independent individuals I have come across all adhered to a spending plan. On the other hand, the ones who talked as if their financial life was under control attempting to live as though they were financially independent, didn't have a spending plan and didn't have any money. Don't be fooled into believing you have it under control and don't be afraid to face your spending habits. By adhering to a spending plan you will be in the top percentage of those that control their finances rather than allow their finances to control them.

True Prosperity

3. Save for the Future

Proverbs 21:20 tells us, "In the house of the wise are stores of choice food and oil, but a foolish man devours all he has." In chapter 13 Solomon says, "He who gathers money little by little makes it grow" (v. 11b). I mentioned in chapter six about saving ten percent of your income regardless of your age. You may think this sounds like a lot. If you have no savings plan at all, it is. However, realize what the ramifications of not saving are. Here are some enlightening facts.

- At the age of 65, 45% of all Americans are dependent on relatives, 30% are dependent on charity, 23% are still working and only 2% are financially independent.
- At age 65, 85 out of 100 Americans don't have $250 in cash.
- 80% of all Americans owe more than then own.
- The Japanese save 15% to 20% of their income. Americans save about 3%.

Not a very pretty picture is it? Our financial future depends on our knowledge and the realization that other than winning the lottery or inheriting money it's up to us to provide for tomorrow. Discipline, persistence and following a savings plan are the key ingredients in making accumulation and financial freedom a reality.

Accumulating wealth no matter how much it may be must begin somewhere. Because of the magic of time and compound interest there is no time like the present. Anyone that has accumulated money in their lifetime with a savings plan realized the importance of compound interest and time being on their side. Let me give you an example of two individuals, one con-

Living Beyond Financial Slavery

tributing to an IRA from the age of 21 to the age of 30 and the other beginning at age 31 and continuing until the age of 60. Both earn at the same interest rate, yet the one contributing for 30 years has less money at the age of 60 than the one that contributes for only ten years because of the magic of time and compound interest.

Put another way, let me ask you this question. Do you believe you could save $6.50 a day—yes or no? When I ask this question in my seminars the answer is almost always a definite *yes*. If it is with you and you're not saving at least that much, why aren't you? Procrastination is the biggest killer of dreams next to fear. Theodore Roosevelt once said, "In a moment of decision, the best thing you can do is the right thing to do. The worst thing to do is nothing."

Consider that $6.50 a day equals approximately $200 per month. At 16% interest in five years you would have $19,000. In ten years the total would be $60,000; 15 years, $150,000; 20, $350,000. In 25 years you would have just under one million dollars.

You are probably saying that all sounds well, but 16% interest? That sounds high. I agree. But did you know that according to data by Morningstar, Inc. the average small cap mutual fund returned 16.9% from 1976-96?

The main excuse people have about saving is that they can't afford to. My answer to that is you can't afford not to. In order to save you need to remain focused, disciplined and refrain from activities on investments that cause you to loose money. A self-made billionaire was asked what his secret to wealth was. His answer was that he has two rules. Rule number one is don't

True Prosperity

loose money. Rule number two is when tempted, refer to rule number one.

I mention this because if you are going to save money you have to refrain from loosing it by remaining focused on your goal. Stay clear of off the wall investment opportunities and develop an accumulation mindset. If regular saving is part of your financial life, that's great. Continue doing so. If it's not, I urge you to make it an integral part of your plan to avoid financial slavery and gain financial freedom. Tomorrow will come faster than you thin,k and you will be glad that you created financial securityr for you life.

4. Enjoy What You Have

There is an old saying that describes contentment in detail in my opinion. It is "use it up, wear it out, make it do or do without." A large percentage of people today are never satisfied with anything in life or with life itself. They simply exist wanting more and more and never enjoying today or what they have. People save to buy something only to be disappointed because by the time they get it a better one exists on the market. This one area I believe causes more disagreements and strife between couples than most any other. "I never can satisfy you! You always want more! No matter what you have, it's never enough!" The statements revolving around contentment go on and on.

Hebrews 13:5 says, "Be content with what you have." Am I saying it's not right to strive to be more, have more, etc.? Absolutely not! What I am saying is that you need to be content with who you are. Go ahead. Shoot for the stars. Set goals as I have explained here. But don't loose sight of today. If tomorrow never comes, today is all you will ever have. Some say contentment leads to laziness. I disagree. Complacency leads to laziness. Contentment and complacency are two totally different things. Realize the true meaning of contentment which is to enjoy the present. Give thanks to God for your blessings regardless of how little or small they may be. Find happiness in who you are today. Practice satisfaction when you purchase an item or meet a goal. Remember that you have everything of which to be glad and nothing of which to be sad.

5. Learn the Importance of Giving
I emphasized this point also in one of my financial principles. It is important in the overall picture of financial health. People everyday talk to me about their financial lives. Ultimately the ones that have very little are bound in financial bondage because they give very little. They justify it by their own philosophy. Proverbs 3:9-10 encourages us to honor the Lord by giving Him the first part of all your income. He will cause "your barns [to] be filled to overflowing."

Proverbs 10:16 reads, "The wages of the righteous bring them life." Chapter 22:9 says, "A generous man will himself be blessed, for he shares his food with the poor." Jesus himself said, "It is more blessed to give than to receive" (Acts 20:35).

Giving without a doubt is the most misunderstood guideline for financial freedom. Many people believe and are being taught that they should give for the reason of receiving something in return. It doesn't work that way. James says, "When you ask, you do not receive, because you ask with wrong motives" (James 4:3). Giving should come from your heart first because we are instructed to do so and second because we

True Prosperity

desire to do so. We should not give to receive, but rather to see that others receive. If we give for the reason of giving then we are giving for the right reason.

John explains, "If we ask anything according to his will, he hears us" (I John 5:14). *According to His will* are the key words in that verse. People are being mislead by well-known preachers telling them to give and claim their Mercedes Benz or whatever their hearts desire.

Hopefully by now you will realize that I am all for you striving and achieving the desires of your heart as long as they are right for you. If you want and can afford a Mercedes Benz, all I can say is more power to you. Just be sure your desire is pure and not to impress others.

That's what I find most humorous among many people when they buy an expensive item. They get it to impress others. Have you ever thought of that? Why would we buy things we don't want with money we don't have to impress people we don't like? I haven't been able to figure that one out.

So how do you know if you qualify to receive for your giving, namely the hundred-fold return spoken of in Mark 10:29–30? How do you know if you are giving for the right reason? Below I have listed three questions to ask yourself when evaluating whether you are giving according to biblical laws:

- Have I really put God first in every area of my life?
- Have I studied the biblical laws of prosperity and am I following them?
- Do I really want financial blessings, not for my own selfish desires, but rather to do His will in my life?

[Source *Moore for your Money*, Byron R Moore, CFP, April 1998]

Living Beyond Financial Slavery

If you answered yes to these questions, you are qualifying for the financial blessing in Mark 10. If not, reevaluate your giving and line them up with these principles. If you give for the right reason, it won't matter if the one you gave abused the money. They will answer for their wrongdoing, not you. In life we reap what we sow. If we want people to be nice to us, we must be nice to them. Many people fail to realize that this same principal works with their finances.

One of the biggest cancers in human nature is greed. It knocks on everyone's door at one time or another. Humanly speaking, you cannot escape it. Spiritually speaking however, you can. If you plant financial seeds regularly during your life it causes that equal and opposite reaction, and greed diminishes. It is very difficult to give regularly and be greedy at the same time. That is, unless you are giving only to receive one-hundred-fold returns on every seed you plant. Here are a few foundational truths important to understand when giving.

First, God doesn't need our money. He wants you to sow seeds for your benefit, not His. Second, if we sow sparingly, you will reap modest rewards. "Remember this, whoever sows sparingly will also reap sparingly, whoever sows generously will also reap generously" (II Corinthians 9:6). Everything we own belongs to God. To give him 10% is a deal when you come to grips with that. God will supply your needs so that we can have enough left over to contribute to other good works.

Finally, we must give cheerfully. "God loves a cheerful giver, and God is able to make all grace abound to you, so that in all things at all times, having all that you need, you will abound in every good work" (II Corinthians 9:7-8).

True Prosperity

Not being a cheerful giver, in my opinion, is the main reason why people do not reap the rewards of their giving. God doesn't have to provide all of the things listed in II Corinthians 9:8. He is able to and will if we give bountifully and cheerfully. This type of giving doesn't just receive back but also helps others with their specific needs. Reaping the benefits of seed faith is a wonderful thing, but it should not be your main purpose. Give and give cheerfully. You will be blessed and have more than enough to meet all of your needs.

6. Expect an Honest Day's Pay For an Honest Day's Work

If we constantly try to get paid more than our work is worth, we are violating the laws of prosperity. We need to work as hard as we possibly can instead of doing as little as possible. "Whatever your hand finds to do, do it with all your might" (Ecclesiastes 9:10).

Learn to go the extra mile. Do more than you are asked to do. Jesus told us to go two miles if we need to go one. "If someone forces you to go with him one mile, go with him two miles" (Matthew 5:41).

7. Realize Hard Work Requires Discipline

If we want freedom from financial problems or any other problems in life, we must be disciplined. Financial discipline, spiritual, physical, mental or emotional discipline is to be developed for success to be achieved. Success achieved without hard work and discipline is artificial and temporary. Only when we discipline ourselves and work hard toward a goal, will our ultimate outcome be real and lasting in nature.

Living Beyond Financial Slavery

8. Avoid Financial Lust of the Eye.
Financial lust of the eye is one of the leading causes of financial slavery today. I hear individuals talking about what others have, what others are doing, and what others are driving. I have a saying for this. Things are seldom as they appear or as they are told when it comes to money. Proverbs 13.7 says, "One man pretends to be rich, yet has nothing: Another pretends to be poor, yet has great wealth."

Most individuals that people lust over have a fraction of what others think they do. As you have learned, success comes in many different forms. I know of no one that is richer than the individual that is loved by his or her family and has a loving relationship with God. Beauty may be only skin deep in some cases, but I can assure you that wealth without love is in all cases. It takes all of the building blocks we have discussed to this point to build true success. I have yet to see anyone desire what another has that has been satisfied with what they found if they pursued it. Life just doesn't worth that way. There is only one Man to follow, one Champion. There is only One that is always a winner. Jesus Christ is that man. If you cast your eyes on Him, you will find that all else pales in comparison.

Understanding these basic guidelines and foundational truths are not the usual worldly way of viewing finances and debt. They are God's ways and I believe in His way far above any man's philosophy. Now that you have the foundation required for avoiding financial slavery, what if you are entrapped in it? How do you become free? First, pray for the strength and will power it takes to avoid the buying game. Second, come to the unwavering position that you have had enough and be willing to make a change. Last learn all you can about finances so that you have a basic understanding of how to handle money. Some people are gifted in this area while others struggle their whole life.

There are many books on the subject of reducing and eliminating debt on the market today. Therefore, I will concentrate on the types of debt and debt traps that we are faced with everyday.

Before proceeding, let me emphasize that unmanageable debt, regardless of what type it is, is not good. Avoid it at all cost by praying and thinking about a purchase before you make it. Is it necessary? Is it something I can do without? Can I manage this debt and pay it off earlier than scheduled?

These are a few of the questions that you should embed in your mind when contemplating a purchase. Take time before buying an impulse item and up to 15 days on major purchases. Most have reported that they decided against what it was they were contemplating buying while the ones that did purchase using this philosophy had few regrets. Only by learning to say *no* can you truly become debt free and only when you strive for this freedom will you experience the financial life that you are capable of having.

Types of Debt

Appreciable debt
This debt is the type of debt that goes up in value. A prime example is real estate. The debt on your home is money owed like any other debt. The difference is the home is increasing in value. This type of debt is the best type to have of the two types.

Living Beyond Financial Slavery

Depreciable debt
This debt is the type of debt that goes down in value. Examples are automobiles, most credit card debt, personal debts, equipment debts, etc. This is the area that most people get themselves into trouble.

I see more young people today than ever before in debt up to their eyeballs with nothing to show for. Pre-approved credit cards are being sent to teenagers before they learn how to pay a phone bill. There are charge limits on the card, but the problem lies in two areas. First, young people have no earthly concept of how to use a credit card. Second, the next pre-approved card has no idea what the last pre-approved cards limit is or, for that matter, how many credit cards the individual has in his or her possession.

Young people are not the only ones that are victims of credit card debt. The second reason above plays a large factor in that. If one cannot receive an approval for $20,000 from a particular credit card company, why should he or she be able to receive ten approvals for $2,000 each from different companies?

The credit industry is fast becoming a major part of our exchange system. The future could very well lead to a totally cashless society. If this becomes reality, it becomes of utmost importance for parents to teach their children the value of a dollar and how to manage debt. Regardless of what kind of debt you have, the danger only comes when you can't manage what you owe. Debt is part of our society. Unmanageable debt is part of our nation and we can't let that filter down to the next generation. We must become cognizant of the debt traps that surround us. Let's take a look at the two main debt traps we confront frequently.

True Prosperity

Credit Card Schemes
Two popular schemes used today are
>   1. Pre-approved cards — discussed above
>   2. No annual fee/low interest rates

I am astounded at how many people fall into this trap. Credit cards are advertising no annual fee or interest rates below the norm. How do you know if you're getting scammed? READ THE FINE PRINT! Most cards waive certain fees and/or lower rates for a short period of time only to resume at a rate equal to or higher than the norm. Reading the fine print will save you much heartache in the future.

Monthly Payment Schemes
I am astounded at the amortization proposals (the way interest and principle are calculated and how your loan payment is applied to reduce them) made on merchandise these days. Not long ago, I was reading an outdoor magazine and happened to turn to the section on boats. It appeared that each boat was offered at a substantial savings reflected in the advertised monthly note. As I read further (especially the fine print), I noticed these boats were amortized over 120 months, a ten-year period! Ten Years! I can't imagine how the individual purchasing one of these boats would feel five or six years later should he wish to sell. The owner would be upside down, owing more than the boat is worth, with another four to five years left on the debt.

Automotive dealerships are guilty of this as well. They offer low monthly rates that are a reflection of long amortization periods or balloon payments at the end. No matter whether you are purchasing an automobile, boat or other merchandise, be sure you understand the terms before signing.

People from all walks of life have been burned. They refuse to admit it because of pride and a lack of diligence, this author included. The time you spend studying the terms involved in your purchase could save you literally thousands of dollars.

Financial slavery is alive and well in America today. It is my hope that this book will assist you in circumventing its nasty claws. Even if you avoid one mistake you would have otherwise made, it's worth it. I urge you to become educated in the financial arena that surrounds you everyday. Whether you are a professional or a blue-collar worker, you will be faced with financial decisions during your lifetime. Avoiding mistakes takes a little time and study, but I can assure you the rewards are well worth it.

11
Following the Long and Narrow

"BUT SMALL IS THE GATE AND NARROW THE ROAD that leads to life, and only a few find it." Matthew 7:14 so vividly expresses to us how to find life. The world is searching for the answer to truth, happiness, success, etc., and it's right under their nose. Allow me to spell it out for you should you have somehow missed it along the way. True success comes from experiencing heartfelt joy. If you are searching for the kind of happiness and fulfillment that lasts for eternity, you need not look any further than the cross of Jesus Christ. Regardless of what denomination you are, what your past is or where in life you now are, you can start a new life by realizing that forgiveness is yours for the asking. The freedom of unforgiveness is beyond question the greatest freedom you will experience in your life. Not many people realize what God has given them.

As we have discussed throughout this book, nothing worthwhile comes easy. Just do nothing. Welcome or not, failure will be sure to visit you.

Did you know the word *success* is mentioned only once in the Bible? If you want to be successful at whatever you do, there are three specific things required. We mentioned them before. You will find these spiritual principles in the following passage of

True Prosperity

Scripture. "Do not let this Book of the Law depart from your mouth; meditate on it day and night, so that you may be careful to do everything written in it. Then you will be prosperous and successful" (Joshua 1:8).

If you read this passage thoroughly, you will see that the instructions on how to achieve prosperity, wisdom and success is a conditional promise. Let's take a look at the three specific instructions given to us in Joshua 1:8.

God's Word should not depart from our mouth. In other words, we should be proud to speak of God constantly. What comes from our mouths is based on what is stored in our hearts. When we fill our minds with the clean, the pure and the positive that comes from the Bible, our hearts will overflow with God. When our hearts overflow, our mouths will follow.

Meditate day and night in the Word of God. We spoke of this in a previous chapter, but it is important to understand this principle. So many people take parts of the Bible seriously and leave other parts out. The Bible is one book, the rulebook of life. Everything you need to know or ever will need to know is contained within its pages. To meditate on the Word means to let it become part of you so that your mouth can speak it clearly when your heart feels it. Meditation in the Word causes it to transfer from our minds to our heart. Matthew 12:34-35 tells us that the words that flow out of our mouths are based on what we have stored in our hearts.

Observe and do according to all that is written in the Word of God. Abide by the laws. If we meditate on a scripture mak-

Following the Long and Narrow

ing it part of our heart and mind, it becomes much easier to live by.

I told you at the beginning of this book that I would tell you what success is and how you can obtain it. I further told you each principle would be based on a solid biblical foundation. So far, so good. Living the successful life can be a different story altogether. It is a long and narrow road. Much of the way we live has to do with attitude.

Therefore, I devised ten attitudes to adhere by for successful living. As you read through them, understand they have been devised from years of watching successful people gain and maintain the success they have achieved. Those that failed violated each of them.

1. Be yourself. Never *act* like you have money regardless of your status.
2. Live within your means. Don't try to be someone you are not.
3. Remember that big isn't always better. Big offices do not reflect big incomes. Neither do big mouths.
4. Think small when it comes to overhead and budgets.
5. Think big when it comes to accomplishments, production and bottom line.
6. Avoid jealousy. Be genuine and happy for others accomplishments.
7. Keep your eyes focused on God. By now you are aware that success comes in all different forms. Model yourself after the One who was perfect in all areas. Allow the Spirit of Christ to work through you.
8. Walk the long and narrow path. Avoid situations that

threaten or tempt you to do things that are immoral or unethical by viewing life from tomorrow rather than today. If your decision could potentially inflict pain on yourself or someone you love, turn away from it. Remember very few things that provide instant gratification in life carry any type of permanent fulfillment with it.

9. Concentrate on the important things in life, the things that last, such as your relationships with God, family and friends. No matter what you accomplish or what you attain, most will not remember what you did when you're gone.

10. Get out of religion and into relationships. God wants all of you on His terms, not that of the Church, manmade rules or opinions. By experiencing a true relationship with God, you will experience true joy and happiness and, in time, personal success will be inevitable.

The difficulty of balancing a life in all areas cannot be overemphasized. Spiritual, family, physical, mental, social life, and so on, takes concentration, patience, faith and perseverance. So many people fail in certain areas of their lives because of too much time spent in others. For instance, I could spend all of my time at work and fail in the area of responsibility for my family. I could spend all of my time at home and watch my family suffer because of financial disaster. I could even spend every waking moment at church and watch my family and career suffer.

I do not think you can overdo your spirituality. In other words, you cannot get too much of God. You can, I believe, get

Following the Long and Narrow

over-churched by being there every waking moment losing out in the other building blocks of life, namely family. Have you ever stopped to think just how difficult it is to balance your life? It seems impossible!

To the human eye, it probably is. To the spiritual eye, nothing is impossible. It can be done by allowing Christ to live through you. You can't become Him no matter how hard you try. He can, however, live through you allowing you to enjoy the things He put on this earth for you. And yes, you can enjoy a successful and prosperous life.

Sometime ago, I was in a conversation about success with a friend. In defining success, he mentioned how the meaning is different to everyone. "Should you build this truck and feel it's a success, you were successful at building this truck," he said. I agreed. As I look back at that conversation, I realize how meaningful that statement was. Success is, as I have stated throughout this book, how you define it for yourself. That is, until you compare it to life in general.

For example, if your business or marriage fails, you can call that successful until the moon turns green and success will never enter the picture. That's why I have given you principles, attitudes, criteria, etc., to find and achieve success as it relates to life.

I run into people everyday that are genuinely happy, but something is missing in their lives. They have all those things I discussed in previous chapters, but they are waiting on God to lead them into a different career or in a different direction. The sad part is they may wait until they meet Him face to face.

God is waiting for us to come to Him. When Christ died on the cross, He hung for all the world to see. He did not come to

True Prosperity

man and give salvation; man has to come to him to receive salvation. He has all of the answers, but we must come to Him to receive them. Then and only then will we receive direction in our life.

Is attaining success in life difficult? Yes. Is living the life more difficult? It can be but when you get on the right track your life will resemble a locomotive. You're headed in the right direction and nothing can stop you.

If you are reading this and believe you are not capable of having success in your life, you are dead wrong. You can and you will if you follow Joshua 1:8. Some authors speak of success as if it were something you buy at a local mall. Anything worthwhile is worth working for. God loves you as much as anyone else on earth. That was a fact of grace I had difficulty coping with for years. How can God love a filthy drunkard lying in a ditch as much as me? Or how can God love me as much as him or her? The answer? He died for all of us.

If you have read all of this book and are still struggling with whether you are worthy of God's love and capable of having success in your life, stop worrying! You are and you can!

Success according to the *Book of Life* is available for everyone. It is the gold at the end of the rainbow, the pearl in the oyster and the diamond in the ruff. With hard work, faith and persistence the reward is worth the effort.

Following the Long and Narrow

12
Personal Guidelines for Sane Living

SANE LIVING MAY SOUND SILLY TO SOME, but to most it is a much sought after way of life. As we complete the puzzle of success, realize that life, although serious in nature, should be lived with joy. Achieving and living personal success is one thing. Doing these things joyfully with sanity is another story altogether. As I prayed and studied about the content of this book, I realized that with all of the principles, truths and guidelines listed, we must have a reference to refer to when times get tough.

The following personal guidelines were written specifically for that purpose. You may wish to hang them on your wall or place them in a conspicuous place that you see everyday. I placed them on my desk in my office. When times get tough or life seems serious and deep, they help me find the reality of life's precious moments. None of us know when our time will come or when the trumpet will blow. We do know that life was given to us for living not worrying.

The reality that the world will someday end should cause us to live and breathe in everything life has to offer, not judge all those around us because they don't see what we see. If we are spiritually accepting of Christ's salvation, it really doesn't matter. We can't change tomorrow and we can't change the end of time in the eyes of God. We can live life in a way pleasing to him, our families and those around us. This, in turn, will

True Prosperity

produce a life pleasing to ourselves. When life is pleasing to us, we become more productive, living our lives the way God intended us to live them.

I hope these guidelines are as meaningful to your life as they have been to mine since God instilled them in my heart.

Personal Guidelines
1. Forgive others as part of the price you pay for being forgiven. Realize that sometimes you are not the most enjoyable person to be around yourself.
2. Balance your life between work and play–seriousness and laughter. Attend church regularly and go to an occasional ball game.
3. Exercise regularly. Get lots of sunshine and fresh air. Occasionally get some rain in your face and dirt on your hands.
4. Stick to the truth no matter how bad it makes you look or feel. Lies are like wandering ghosts.
5. Have a friend you trust. Talk about your troubles, mistakes and your dreams too.
6. Find some quiet time to think. Give time to God and don't underestimate the ability of prayer.
7. Face your fears head-on. Learn which ones are useful and which ones are not.
8. Always remember the ultimate death rate remains 100%. You would be getting short-changed if everyone got to die and you didn't.
9. Learn to relax. When you can't sleep, use it as a chance for creative thinking and thanking God for life's

Personal Guidelines for Sane Living

blessings.

10. Realize there is nothing more precious than life. Fall in love with children, the outdoors, older people, music, books, new places, and the ocean—with everything, except money.

If you look at each of these guidelines closely, you will realize a view of life without the rose-colored glasses. Seeing life for what it is and knowing how to cope with it is the key to successful living. By now success has become a regular word in our vocabulary.

I would like to tell you an American success story. This person lived the successful life most have only dreamed of. You see the creation of his dream with the colors red, white and blue on top of cars throughout America. Chances are, most of you have partaken of his products at least once before. His company was the first to offer fast food delivery of its product. Similar businesses across America felt its impact as expansion ultimately came. Its success revoled around speed and quality. Hungry? Call them and they will deliver to your door with seemingly unbeatable and unstoppable service. The business? Domino's Pizza. The success story? Thomas S. Monaghan, founder and 97 percent owner.

Monaghan and his brother reportedly borrowed $900 to start this business. Within a short period of time, their company began to achieve a successful history. Monaghan targeted collegiate towns in New England and the pizza chain grew so rapidly that in 1985, the company had opened nine hundred stores—a record for a restaurant chain in a single year.

Almost overnight, Thomas Monaghan was a millionaire—a real millionaire. He was the kind that could buy anything he

True Prosperity

wanted. He purchased the Detroit tigers that won the World Series the next year. Monaghan bought about two hundred automobiles including a 1929 Bugatti Royale, which alone cost 8.1 million. He collected airplanes and paid for a lodge located on 3,000 acres of land. The land came complete with an airstrip, hanger and a 580-foot pier on a lake where he floated a couple of yachts.

This $30 million possession eventually boasted a championship golf course, bowling alley, and hotel. He eventually began to finance missions and mission projects to Honduras. Funding missions gave him such enjoyment that he considered selling his company to do philanthropic work full time.

Monaghan was so busy chasing dreams and visions that he failed to notice the need to seriously revise some of his company's business practices. Competitions such as Pizza Hut and Little Caesar's did notice and quickly expanded taking a greater share of the market. Domino's sales began to drop and some stores had to be closed.

If I were to ask you what happened with the remainder of this story, you may be able to answer correctly. In Monaghan's words, "I'd taken my eye off of the ball." That may be a vital part of what happened, but the true problem revolved around priorities.

One night he read a book by C.S. Lewis titled *Mere Christianity*. By the eighth chapter, Monaghan realized he was full of the deadliest of all sins—pride. He had spent years building, buying and enjoying anything he wanted. He decided to stop building his dream home, sell his cars, planes and other belongings.

God had touched Monaghan. He testified from that point on he would focus on God first, then family and finally

Personal Guidelines for Sane Living

Domino's. The rest is history. Today Domino's operates stores in thirty-eight countries and around the world with profits in 1993 of at least $3 million a month.

Success, almost disaster, incredible success again. What had happened? Success came from an entrepreneur filled with a dream. Near disaster came when the man allowed himself to be distracted by the rewards of success. Renewed success came because he prioritized his life focusing on doing one thing well rather than being distracted by so many others.

Priorities are easy to shuffle around and the results of that shuffling can be detrimental. I too, have been caught up in the success web and nearly gobbled up by the spider of destruction. It may not happen immediately, but without prioritizing your life correctly, you will eventually lose in the game of success. I can remember when nothing else really mattered to me other than obtaining my goals in business. I would have never admitted that, but actions spoke louder than words. Many nights were spent on my knees wondering if I was going to lose it all. Rapid expansion into over twenty health care offices had left us undercapitalized and headed for disaster.

Only when I faced the problem head-on and placed my priorities back in the right place did my life change. Today God has richly blessed my life with a beautiful wife, family, home and successful businesses. Most of all He has given me peace and internal fulfillment. That's something that no one can take away from you.

If you desire true personal success in your life, you need to first know the *rules of life*. With practically everything we buy, there is an instruction manual included. You can try to build it, operate it, and make it function as you desire it to, but without

True Prosperity

following the manufactures instruction manual, you will ultimately fail. This may occur before or after you operate it. Not knowing how something is structured, realizing how it functions or understanding what to avoid, causes problems in the life and operation of the item in question.

So also are our lives. Our instruction manual is the Bible. The *rules of life* are found there. The words and principles in the Bible always lead to life. They do not mislead us or tell partial truths. They are the total truth because they are from God. To know the rules of life read the Bible.

Second, live by the *rules of life*. Most Christians are familiar with the rules of life found in the Bible. Living by them is a much greater challenge. The rules laid out for us are our parameters. As long as we live by them, we can win at the game of life. Many biblical figures knew the *rules of life*, yet many believed God would make exceptions to them. You know the stories.

Everyone plays by the same rulebook and everyone is responsible to live by the instructions therein. These rules, or instructions, will always lead you to life and peace. They are truth.

Last, keep our eyes focused in the right direction. Close the door to all other detractions that will come your way. Many people achieve success in life living by the rulebook only to allow their eyes and minds to look in the wrong direction. In small steps they turn from the successful to the one seemingly more enjoyable. Eventually they fall. And all for what? To pursue something they thought would bring more happiness, more success, more of what seems to be what they want until they get it. Then everything changes. They want what they had before and can't understand why it can't be achieved in the

Personal Guidelines for Sane Living

same way again. "God forgives all sins," they say. "So why hasn't He forgiven me?"

The answer is, He has. The problem most people do not want to face is that although all sin is forgiven, we must pay the consequences. That is something none of us want to do. If you smoke, you must pay the physical consequences. If you over drink, you must pay the physical consequences. If you cheat in business or in your marriage, you must pay the consequences. Forgiveness does not preclude that fact.

I pursued financial success to the extreme. When I woke up, I ran for the goal in front of me. When I went to bed at night, I ran in my mind for the finish line. When things were going well, I ran. When things began falling apart, I ran. When my family revealed they were neglected, I ran. Know what I did when my wife said she would like to spend more time with me? I kept on running. Running toward a goal that I thought would bring me happiness, fulfillment and joy. I thought it would bring my family that as well. How wrong I was.

Should I have continued running, I would have never reached the finish line. Most people that run without proper priorities, outside the parameters of the *rules of life*, just keep on running and never stop. They never attain what it is they are looking for even if they are lucky enough to reach the much sought after finish line. True success takes much more than that. It takes all of the things described in this book. Simplistically speaking, it takes Jesus.

As I bring our time together to a close, I would like to leave you with a poem. I thought it would sum up what we have been studying about achieving and maintaining success.

True Prosperity

> ## Success Takes Thee
>
> Success takes thee to be complete;
> It's not enough to just compete.
> You must pursue success with love
> By love's Creator, God above.
>
> Then your life will be firm and strong;
> Able to last when things go wrong.
> Because you experienced God's love and know
> He's always there, He'll never go.
>
> And you have loved Him in kind
> with all the heart and soul and mind;
> And in that love you've found the way.
> To experience success every day.
>
> A life that follows God's plan
> Takes more than just a woman or a man.
> It needs a oneness that can be
> Only from Christ—success takes thee.

Be an Example
As individuals seeking success, we have a duty to be examples for others to follow. We have a duty to give our children and those we come in contact with a role model to follow. When we provide a clear role model, we are paving the way of how to

Personal Guidelines for Sane Living

function in this world. It is my God-appointed task to insure that my children will be ready to lead a family. I have two sons that must be ready to lead a family in the next generation. They are the fathers of tomorrow. All of my children must know whom they are and what they are to do. They must see a role model in action.

It's our job to save our next generation. Regardless of how much success we achieve in life, if we lose sight of that, it's all in vain.

What we leave for others to follow will make the difference in their lives and the lives of others. I have five goals for saving my children. It is my prayer that you join me in grasping these goals. I pray you live an example life that produces success beyond anything you could ever achieve, the kind that lasts for eternity.

Five Goals for Saving My Children
1. To know and obey Jesus Christ
2. To display godly character
3. To display love to my wife
4. To display love to my children
5. To let them see my gifts and abilities, my strengths and weaknesses, so I can work hard and effectively in an area of strength, rather than weakness, and contribute to the lives of others while having fun at the same time

May God's marvelous love, as fresh as the morning and sweet as the dew rest and abide upon you always as you reach for the stars while keeping your eyes focused on the one true star of all—Jesus Christ.